EXCITING REVIEWS

FOR
MARLIN BREE
BOOKS

"Will set your teeth on edge."
– Rocky Mountain News

"An adventure — he encountered several fierce storms
– and an anecdotal history of the lake with tidbits
on Indians, voyageurs, miners, sea captains ...
as well as tales of wind, weather icy
(and sometimes frozen) water, and shipwrecks.
— Booklist

"Bree and his Persistence dared greatly, struggled greatly,
and had a worthy run, told with touching candor.
Bree is at his best when the lake was at its worst."
– Wilmington Evening Journal

"A voyageur's tale of sailing solo, occasionally
in dangerous dark seas, on Lake Superior.
A lovingly written story."
– Baltimore Sun

"Captures the feel and wild spirit of one of the most beautiful
but treacherous bodies of water in the world."
– Star–Tribune, Minneapolis

"A fascinating and exciting story of one man's
adventures on Lake Superior."
– Books for Travel

"...fascinating, informative, entertaining
and totally engaging books that are
a 'must' for anyone who has ever sailed
Lake Superior – or wanted to."
– Wisconsin Bookwatch

BOOKS
BY
MARLIN BREE

WAKE
OF THE
GREEN STORM
A Survivor's Tale

IN THE TEETH
OF THE
NORTHEASTER
A Solo Voyage on Lake Superior

CALL
OF THE
NORTH WIND
Voyages and Adventures
on Lake Superior

BOAT LOG
& RECORD

ALSO

BY GERRY SPIESS
WITH MARLIN BREE

ALONE
AGAINST
THE
ATLANTIC

WAKE OF THE GREEN STORM

A Survivor's Tale

MARLIN BREE

MARLOR PRESS
Saint Paul
Minnesota

W A K E
O F   T H E
G R E E N
S T O R M

Copyright 2001
By MARLIN BREE

Illustrations by Marlin Bree
All photographs throughout the book were taken
by the author unless otherwise credited
Published by Marlor Press, Inc.

ISBN 1-892147-04-1

Printed in the United States of America
Distributed to the book trade in the USA
By Independent Publishers Group, Chicago
Cover design by Mighty Media

First Edition

Library of Congress Cataloging-in-Publication Data

Bree, Marlin, 1933-
Wake of the green storm : a survivor's tale / Marlin Bree. -- 1st ed.
p.cm.
Includes index.
ISBN 1-892147-04-1
1. Storms -- Superior, Lake. 2. Superior, Lake -- Description and travel.
3. Bree, Marlin, 1933 --- Journeys, Lake. 4/ Sailing -- Superior, Lake. I. Title.
F552.B77 2001
917.13'12--dc21   2001016233

MARLOR PRESS, INC.
4304 Brigadoon Drive
Saint Paul, MN 55126

*Dedicated
to*

*Loris
& Will*

*My Own
Safe
Harbor*

*Draw your chair up close
to the edge of the precipice,
and I'll tell you a story.*

— F. Scott Fitzgerald

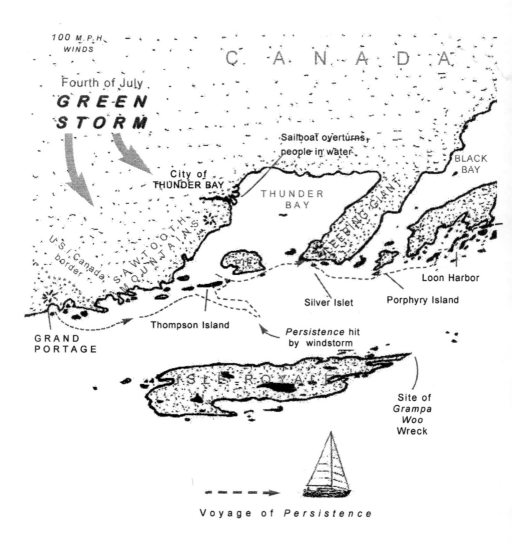

100 M.P.H. WINDS

Fourth of July

GREEN STORM

CANADA

Sailboat overturns, people in water

City of THUNDER BAY

THUNDER BAY

BLACK BAY

SLEEPING GIANT

U.S. Canada border

SAWTOOTH MOUNTAINS

THE

Silver Islet

Porphyry Island

Loon Harbor

GRAND PORTAGE

Thompson Island

Persistence hit by windstorm

ISLE ROYALE

Site of *Grampa Woo* Wreck

Voyage of *Persistence*

L A K E

U N I T S O F

Nautical mile = 1.15 statute miles (in terms of boat speed, measured as nautical miles per hour (knots.) *Nautical mile* = 1.85 kilometers *Miles per hour* (m.p.h.) = 1.609 kilometers per hour (kph)

NORTH

NIPPIGON BAY

ROSSPORT

To Gold Fields

Moss Island

CPR Harbor

Simpson Island

Persistence runs up on reefs

Guinilda shipwreck

Island of Doom

AREA SHOWN ABOVE

SLATE ISLANDS

Thunder Bay

Rossport

Grand Portage

Duluth

LAKE SUPERIOR

Apostle Islands

Saulte Ste. Marie

S U P E R I O R

M E A S U R E M E N T   AS USED IN THE BOOK

Statute mile = 1,609 meters *Kilometer* = .609 of a mile In speed, measured as kilometers per hour (kph) *Fathoms* = 6 feet
For example, 30 knots of wind equals 34.5 m.p.h. (30 x 1.15)

PERSISTENCE

Anatomy of a Small Sailboat

Length overall: 20 feet

Beam: 7 feet, 4 inches

Draft: Centerboard up, 12 inches. CB down, 4 feet, 6 inches

Sail area: Main, 80 sq. ft; Jib. 88 sq. ft.

Sail handling: Main has 2 reefing points and is fully battened. Jib is set on furler with controls to cockpit

Construction details:
  Keel & stem: white oak. **Ribs**: Mahogany composite. **Hull:** Three layers of 1/8-inch Western Red Cedar veneers, epoxy glued and coated. **Bottom**: Covered with 6-oz. fiberglass cloth, coated with epoxy and carbon. **Finishing**: Hull topside is bright finished with UV- resistant varnish. Bottom has teflon anti-fouling

Electrical: Two solar panels atop cabin recharge two 12-volt marine batteries under forward bunk

Engine: 5 h.p. Nissan outboard mounted on swing bracket. For this wilderness voyage, an additional 5 h.p.engine was fitted to starboard as a "backup."

Radios: VHF radio with mast-head antenna; Ham-band radio; AM/FM radio

Berths: Double berth located in forecastle; two quarterberths aft with storage underneath

Miscellaneous equipment: Magellan GPS, knot meter, depthsounder, three compasses. Portable head (toilet) that fits under forward berth. Foam floatation fore and aft; mast is foamed and sealed. Lightning grounded. Autohelm with remote control

Design additions: Folding cloth dodger fitsover hatch. Portable seat fits under hatch area. Transom lengthened with "scoop." Six-inch deep stub keel added through which centerboard slides up and down

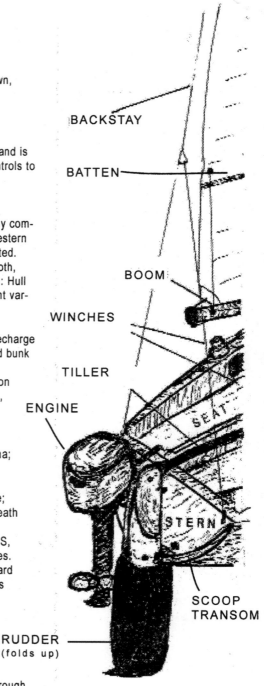

BACKSTAY

BATTEN

BOOM

WINCHES

TILLER

ENGINE

SEAT

STERN

SCOOP TRANSOM

RUDDER
(folds up)

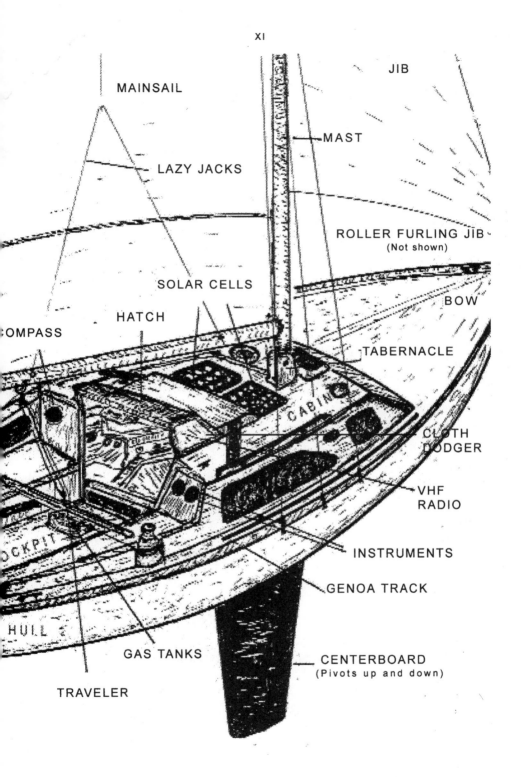

MAINSAIL

JIB

MAST

LAZY JACKS

ROLLER FURLING JIB
(Not shown)

SOLAR CELLS

BOW

HATCH

COMPASS

TABERNACLE

CABIN

CLOTH
DODGER

VHF
RADIO

INSTRUMENTS

COCKPIT

GENOA TRACK

HULL

GAS TANKS

CENTERBOARD
(Pivots up and down)

TRAVELER

CONTENTS

Part Three

EPILOGUE
TO A
VOYAGE

Lake Superior, the largest freshwater
lake in the world, is the northernmost,
westernmost, highest and deepest
of the five Great Lakes.
The shores of the lake are generally
high, rocky and forested.
Thunderstorms can occur at any time
...as isolated single cells or in violent
squall lines. They can generate strong
gusty winds and hail.
On occasion, tornadoes or waterspouts
have been associated with these squalls.
Winds in thunderstorms have been
recorded at around 80 knots.
The lake is large enough for strong winds
from any direction to have sufficient fetch
to build up ... seas of 25 to 30 feet.

— Excerpts from the
United States Coast Pilot

Prologue

STORM
OUT OF
NOWHERE

THE SKY WAS TURNING an ominous blue black. Between
bursts of static, the VHF radio already had called out a
hurried, "*Security, security.*"

Something was coming at me.

A warning snap of wind caught my mast, oscillating it in the
water. My boat shivered.

I looked around. On my port side, Spar Island was a low,
wind-swept piece of rocky desolation.

No refuge there.

To starboard were the notorious open waters of Lake Superior.

"Mayday! Mayday!" A new call boomed from the radio. Somewhere north of me, a boat had capsized. People were struggling in the water.

The first drops of rain pelted down, heavy and cold. From out of nowhere, something unholy grabbed my mast and shook my whole boat beneath it.

A heavy, continuous blast slammed into us — a solid wall of wind. The boat skittered along the waves, faster and faster.

We were headed out into Superior. Anything could happen now.

With a sudden jolt, the boat slewed sideways in the water, tripped and stopped. I was thrown on my side, feet above my head, a pain circling through my ribs. Above me, the starboard portlight turned a vivid green.

It was underwater!

The boat lay helpless, beam to the wind — the most dangerous position. The steering no longer worked, and the engine racketed insanely, its prop out of the water.

We were teetering, balancing on the edge of survival.

"Please!" I implored my boat.

The wind bulked up behind the hull and *Persistence* canted further to one side.

I could feel the chill of the icy waters on my face.

We were turning over, slowly, oh, so slowly.

I braced myself.

This is it! We're going over!

Part One

OUTWARD BOUND

Ashore forever? No, Never!
So long as this life does last,
So long as my heart has passions,
I must ship before the mast

Chapter One

DREAMS OF
THE ISLANDS

Twenty years from now, you will be more disappointed by the things
that you didn't, than by the ones you did do. So throw off the bow lines.
Sail away from the safe harbor. Catch the trade winds in your sails.
Explore. Dream. Discover.
—Mark Twain

IN MY MIND'S EYE, I could see it already: a green island arising from blue waters, with lofty peaks wreathed in mists — resembling something out of the South Pacific.

It was beckoning to me.

My own special island. I stood in my cockpit to get a better view, shading my eyes with my hands.

Verdant trees stretched from the water's edge up steep, roundels of hills. All was hushed. The island seemed still and mysterious.

As I sailed nearer, the water shimmered like a mirror. The sky glittered in blue, laced with soft white clouds. In the crystal waters, rocks glided mesmerizingly under my keel.

I felt a sense of awe.

It was like entering a church and ...

*   *   *

My telephone rang, and once again I was snapped back to reality. I was not cruising Lake Superior but was in my publishing office.

Duty called.

But later that afternoon, I walked to my workroom where I had 24 charts of Lake Superior. Motes of dust arose as I unrolled the charts I needed.

I knew where I wanted to be.

I'd sailed most of Superior —- but I had saved the best for last.

I was looking at a special place I'd dreamed of cruising — a remote and wild archipelago of islands that lay in the northernmost arc of Lake Superior. They extended northeast from Grand Portage, near the border, to about a third of the way up the wild Canadian coastline.

Hundreds of islands! Beautiful islands, remote and serene— green hillocks rising from the inland sea — bearing a spectacular magnificence, with high bluffs, bright coves and ancient beaches.

These islands were one of boating's better kept secrets — except to local boaters. Some sailors knew about them, but not many got into them. From what I'd heard, you could sail up there for days without seeing another boat.

It was a wilderness sailing paradise with its sheltered and isolated waters — a little bit of heaven for anyone who would like a lot of natural beauty and solitude.

*   *   *

For years, I'd been putting off my cruise into this island wilderness. But I found a special urgency: the publicity spotlight was shining to make it the world's largest freshwater conservation area — more than 10,000 square kilometers in size.

Clearly, now was the time to see it, while it was still pristine — an ancient, natural world, not yet overrun by civilization. I leaned back in thought. I could picture myself ambling among the ancient islands, enjoying the summer warmth and light airs.

Not only were these islands a unique wilderness archipelago, they were a link in a remarkable story.

From ancient times, the islands had been part of a birch-bark canoe route from the western shores of what is now Minnesota to the religious grounds at the easternmost part of the lake.

Across these waters paddled the colorful voyageurs, those bold boatmen of hundreds of years ago. As an amateur historian, I wanted to retrace the voyageurs' route as they paddled through the islands.

I would sail in their historic wake.

As I studied my charts, I saw that I'd have some time on the open waters of Superior — always a risk — but if I planned it right I'd mostly be in the protection of the islands. I could sail between channels or behind the island chains, and if a storm started to threaten, I could duck into one of their protected coves or natural harbors.

The hardest part, it seemed to me, would be getting the boat ready and taking time away from my business. I needed to carve out lots of time both to prepare my boat and to make the voyage.

We were both in pretty good shape, but I was age 66. My home-built wooden boat was nearly 22 years old. Neither of us was exactly new and we both had a lot of hard miles on us.

Ahead of us lay the most rugged part of a notoriously stormy body of water.

It would be a special challenge.

Chapter Two

GETTING READY

Will anyone dare to tell me that business is
More entertaining than fooling among boats?
—Robert Louis Stevenson

THE HATCHWAY was the problem this year. When I pressed my thumb into one of the side frames that was supposed to be solid mahogany, the area dented and crumbled.

Rot.

Wood was great for a boat. It was lightweight, it was beautiful, and it could be shaped. But it had to be protected from sunlight or else its finish of varnish and epoxy would crumble away. And if rainwater got in and remained, the result would be rot.

During her 22 years, the little sailboat had been pounded by storms, soaked by rain, and knifed her way through a million waves.

In places, sun had blistered her varnish and water had crept in — now she was having a touch of rot.

Just another task for the dedicated wooden boat owner. I had built my sailboat from the keel up. That meant I could fix her.

*   *   *

The rot was straightforward to fix. Chop, grind, and claw out the crumbling wood; carve a new piece to fit and then replace. Liberally slather on the epoxy.

One job finished. I checked further. The bilge was in good shape, but I was having a problem with wood delamination.

Veneers[1] in the cabin top and on part of the deck had begun to separate and curl around the edges. This was more cosmetic than structural. With my heat gun, I softened the epoxy. Using wood chisels and infinite patience, I scraped the coating off every square inch of cabin top and deck —- murderously hard work.

After I patched in some wood pieces, I sanded the area and covered everything with six-ounce fiberglass cloth. Carefully, I coated epoxy over the fine mesh.

A little miracle happened. As the epoxy wet out the fiberglass and sank into the wood, the surface became transparent. The beauty of the teak and the mahogany glowed. Pleased, I laid on four coats of marine varnish.

"How's the work going?" Loris asked.

"It's wood, ain't it?" This was my standard joking reply.

To which I quickly added, "It's rebuilt — and better than new." My wife understood.

She knew I meant it, too. When I worked on a piece that had broken, failed, or rotted, I made certain to rebuild or replace it stronger and better.

That was important — where I was headed.

*   *   *

I'd been on Superior many times and had already partly circumnavigated the big lake. I knew what to expect. Bouts of heavy weather. Storms. High winds and seas.

This time, I wanted to make my trip a little easier.

Under sail, *Persistence*
(right) has an open cockpit.
Below, the cloth dodger
snaps atop the hatchway,
giving the author just
enough room to sit with his
head sticking up to see
through the windshield.
This inside steering position is equipped with clock,
two compasses (one has to
be right), and a GPS.
Hanging below a folded up
chart is the remote control
for the autopilot. Side panels snap out, and, a back
panel unrolls down over
the hatch boards, giving
the author protection in foul
weather.

When I sat in the open cockpit on long solo voyages, I got sunburned and overheated in the sunshine. In rain, I got soaked and water logged; in cold, chilled. In storms, high winds whipped into me; spray and green water slapped me in the face. Misery.

No more.

Since late winter, I'd been working on my own design for a dodger. This removable, folding cloth covering, not unlike the hood on a baby buggy, would fasten atop the hatch.

I'd sit inside the dodger with my head and shoulders sticking out of the hatch area. I had carved a special wooden seat that I could straddle like a giant bicycle seat at the end of the centerboard trunk.

Come what might in Superior weather — and there was always something nasty brewing up there — I'd be inside and protected.

I even figured out a way to steer my boat from my inside steering station. To my tiller, I attached a small autopilot. To that steering device, I snapped in a remote control, which led to me. When I punched a button, the Autohelm happily buzzed the course correction.

For navigating while I was inside, I added a GPS (global positioning system) and an additional compass. Together with the compass on the turtle about a foot from my nose, I had two compasses to check, figuring that one of them would be right. A clip hanging from a screw-head let me display a folded-down chart in front of me and a little ledge held my dividers, a ruler, and a pen.

I found that my inside steering station was cozy, since my nose was only inches from the forward "windshield" of the dodger. But now I could run my boat and navigate from inside— a major improvement on being in the open cockpit and getting rained on.

I pondered one more problem. An "iron wind" was all-important for safety, even on a sailboat. On another Superior outing, my outboard had broken and I never forgot the trouble I got into.[2]

As a precaution, I hung another five-horsepower engine on the transom. Now I had two five-horsepower engines. If one kicker stalled out, or got temperamental, I had a spare engine — not a bad plan for a wilderness passagemaking on the world's greatest lake.

*   *   *

As the deadline for leaving approached, the work to outfit my little boat seemed to magnify. Time also seemed to shrink.

Problems escalated as I stuffed sailing gear, safety gear, sails, and navigation supplies into the cabin. In it also went food for weeks of wilderness cruising, including juice, bottled water, cereal, powdered milk, canned goods, and three types of coffee. I piled in my clothing, sleeping bags, blankets, pillows and miscellaneous gear.

I also found room for anchors, fenders, lines, gas, oil, and pots and pans. I joked that people could replicate the living space[3] inside my cabin by jacking up their dining room table on telephone directories. Then they could crawl underneath and live there for a month.

I checked out my safety gear. I carried a safety harness that linked me with heavy metal shackles and a nylon strap to an eye-bolt beside the hatchway. I had a Sterns survival suit, the kind with nylon on both sides and a quarter inch of foam neoprene in the center. I also carried personal floatation devices (life preservers), as well as heavy duty foul weather gear.

I added an EPIRB for safety — an emergency position indicating radio beacon. In a last-ditch emergency, such as if I were capsized and being swept out into the lake, I could flip a switch and the EPIRB would broadcast a signal to a satellite so rescuers could send help. EPIRBs are widely used by boaters doing ocean passage making and have saved lives. For sailing Superior, it seemed like a good safety precaution.

Though I carried three radios, including an AM-FM and a Ham-band transceiver, my most useful radio would be my 20-year-old VHF. I had mounted the very high frequency transceiver antenna atop my mast for maximum line-of-sight range, about 26 miles. With it, I could talk with other boats. On this trip I hoped to stay in communication with the Thunder Bay Coast Guard, through its radio repeaters high atop the rugged Canadian coastline.

I looked over my old boat trailer and replaced its tires with a larger size to be sure I had adequate load capacity.

I checked and double checked my to-do list.

Finally, late one evening, I stepped back to inspect. With all the food, gear, and equipment aboard my boat, I thought my trailer's tires bulged outward.

Chapter Three

UP THE
SHORE

The North Shore is in view, an unending range of hills and mountains,
indented here and there with beetling crags and frowning precipices.
Nature here is not in her pretty moods, toying with water.
—Chicago Tribune, 1870

I SNICKED my 1992 Suzuki Sidekick into four-wheel drive, selected the super-low gear, and slowly backed the fully loaded *Persistence* out onto the quiet Shoreview neighborhood street. It was Tuesday, June 29.

My plan was to leave early with Loris, cruise throughout the day and end up in the late afternoon at Grand Portage, Minnesota, just a few miles south of the Canadian border. There, we'd slip the boat into the water, get her rigged and tested, and then I'd depart on my solo voyage on Superior.

I knew it was unlikely that I wouldn't come across some sort of Superior storm, but this time I was going early to be in the optimum window of opportunity for sailing Superior. I'd set sail throughout July and maybe even early August, but be off the lake by September, when storms rolled in and the lake could no longer be trusted.

There would be some sailing on the open waters, but the Canadian islands offered a number of harbors of refuge for small boats. I figured I'd move from island to island, not unlike the sailing I'd done in Superior's beautiful Apostle Islands.

If a storm threatened, I'd duck behind an island or into a cove. In fact, the whole expedition seemed a lot like going into a new, bigger set of Apostles Islands. Or so I thought.

*   *   *

The trip north on Hwy. 35 to Duluth was uneventful but slow under bright sunshine and blue skies. In the small sport-utility vehicle, we cruised pleasantly at about 55 to 60 m.p.h., slowing as we downshifted to get up the hills surrounding Duluth.

Superior spread out in a shimmering sheet of blue water — stretching to infinity on the horizon, blending in to the sky. If you looked closely, you could see a slight bend in the curvature of the inland sea.

I always thought of Superior as a sea — a vast freshwater sea. To think of Superior as merely a lake would be to underestimate its power and its storms. For a small-boat sailor, that could be dangerous.

Beyond Duluth, we climbed along Superior's rugged North Shore on Hwy. 61, leading to the Canadian border. The scenery changed as we came into the Sawtooth Mountains, with steep slopes and cliffs rising 900 feet above the lake. Here the shore is bold and rocky — and inhospitable to the boater.[1]

Looking out over Superior, you gain a real sense of the immense power of this body of fresh water that stretches nearly 400 miles to the east.

A gust of wind swept off the lake and made the four-by-four's canvas top rattle.

*   *   *

Everything was going according to plan. I began to relax as I thought ahead.

At Grand Portage, in the shadows of the legendary mountains, we'd slip *Persistence* into the cold waters of Superior.

Taking a break: Loris stands beside *Persistence* on its trailer.

Grand Portage Bay was about five miles southwest of the international boundary.

I had telephoned ahead to find out which marina I could use to launch *Persistence*, but was told that because of the low levels of the lake this year, I could not use the marina on the northwest side.

I'd start at the marina near Hat Point. I was told that the passenger ferry, the *Voyageur*, operated out of this marina, and sure, I could launch and have a clear path to leave. This was attractive to me since the bay was dotted with shoals and reefs, made even closer to the surface with this year's low water levels.

* * *

By late afternoon, the sun had faded behind heavy clouds. Outside my speeding window, Lake Superior spread out in a vast entity of gray water and dark horizon.

A road sign pointed downward: Grand Portage.

I slipped the four-wheeler into second gear and we began our descent. The wooden stockade of a historic old fur fort came into view. We turned left, following a winding road to the Voyageur's Marina. Several miles later, we pulled into a large, graveled parking area that led down to the landing.

The day had changed from bright sunshine to gray. There was a heavy mass of clouds overhanging the hills.

I stepped out of the vehicle when a wind blast hit me. I clutched my hat to my head, glancing around.

The harbor water became dark and flipped up whitecaps. Boats tied along the dock began a dance with the waves.

A sudden storm had descended.

From the marina office, someone popped her head out the door.

"Where did that come from?" she asked, shaking her head at the sky.

I should have paid more attention.

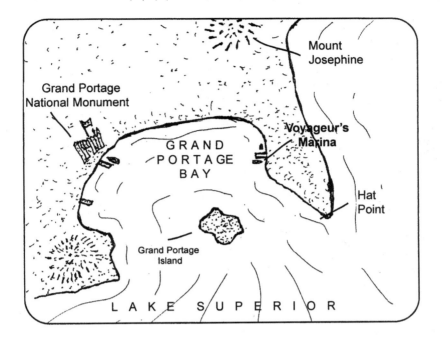

Chapter Four

FOG-BOUND
AT GRAND PORTAGE

The journey is the reward
—Old Taoist Saying

Early-morning fog shrouded nearby Grand Portage Island, coating the lake with blue gray, but here in the harbor, the sun was out and shining brightly. We had *Persistence* off her trailer, bobbing merrily in the water, and loaded with the supplies and provisions from the 4 by 4.

Little *Persistence* seemed to squat in the water in anticipation. But she and I were not going anywhere until the weather improved. The unsettled weather that had blown in yesterday was going to hang on for a while.

It was a different story for my life partner and fellow sailor, who needed to return. "Take care out there," Loris advised me for the umpteenth time.

"I will," I said. "I'll try to sail only in good weather. If it turns bad, I just won't go out."

"And if it gets bad when you're out?"

"I'll duck into an island, somewhere. There are a lot of islands ahead."

I was trying to be positive and I knew she'd be concerned. We'd both logged enough time on Superior to know how unpredictable the weather could be.

"I'll check the forecast before I take off," I added. "And I've got a new barometer."

I felt a tug of loneliness — and pride — as I watched my wife, my 4 by 4 and my trailer disappear up the pine-enclosed road. I was on my own. If I did not like it, I had no one to blame but myself.

I returned to the "pocket," where Kek Melby, the manager at the marina, told us to moor the boat. It turned out to be a slot behind a large wooden break wall and in front of a rusty barge.

This well-protected area of quiet water would be my home at Grand Portage for the next couple of days until the unsettled weather cleared up. I couldn't navigate safely with all the fog out there.

The time I'd spend in port would give me a chance to catch up on some historical research. For want of a better term, I figured I'd be doing a "heritage sail" — trying to reconstruct and understand some of the history that went before me.

I'd follow the track of the voyageurs as they came from New France in their birch-bark canoes. I'd be visiting some of their landing sites in the wilderness and also be following the routes of some shipwrecks on my way along the northernmost island archipelago.

This area was loaded with history.

Here, especially. All I had to do was pop my head out of the hatch and look across the bay to the old fur fort's gleaming stockade.

Chapter Five

HUZZA! LES VOYAGEURS

*No water, no weather, ever stopping
the paddle or the song.
—Voyageur's saying*

IN THE SHADOW of Mt. Josephine, the old fur fort's gleaming stockade nestled along the edge of the harbor.

As I looked across the bay, I tried to imagine what a welcome sight Grand Portage must have been as the voyageurs ended their 1,200-mile watery route from New France. Here was their destination nearly 200 years ago — the very edge of civilization — after paddling and portaging their fragile canoes halfway across a wilderness continent.

Crossing Superior, they braved storms, high waves, and unpredictable weather in birch-bark canoes. These were not Indian-style craft, but 40-foot-long canoes, large enough to hold a dozen men and tons of cargo, yet light enough to carry across the 36 portages between Montreal and Grand Portage.

The heavily loaded canoe brigades set out early each May to carry goods into the wilderness.

Their route lay along the great arc of the lake on the Canadian north shore — the one I would be sailing.

For their deeds, the voyageurs were idolized throughout the world. Legends grew not only about their stamina and strength, but for their bravery in the face of hardship and danger. Stories were told and retold around campfires about how they reveled in harsh adventures, ignored pain and suffering, and literally laughed in the face of danger.

In my mind's eye I can picture them — men big shouldered and heavily muscled from paddling canoes. They'd be talking and laughing, their distinctive long caps twitching from side to side – a jolly bunch, outlandish in their jokes and tales.

"You look like a voyageur," someone once told me. At 5 foot 7 inches, I am not the tallest of guys.

"Except," my friend added, "you should be twice as wide in the shoulders."

He did not add that if I were a typical voyageur, at my age, I'd be suffering from a hernia, chronic back pain, joint aches, or — most likely — be dead.

*   *   *

As I walked through the fur fort's gate, I looked around at the distinctive wooden stockade walls. These were high and had sharpened points at the tops. But the stockade and the log buildings inside the heavy walls were all replicas. The original fort has long since fallen into dust.

The original fur trading post began in 1768, about the time of the American Revolution, and became the inland headquarters of the Montreal fur-trading organization, the North West Company.

I met David Cooper[1], who was with the National Park Service and stationed here at Grand Portage National Monument.

"Native people were using Grand Portage hundreds to thousands of years prior to arrival of Europeans," Cooper told me. He was now talking about the "grand portage," known as the old Great Carrying Place, a largely uphill, rugged nine-mile trail to the waterways leading deep into Canada. "The Indians used it for trading purposes and for seasonal movement. There was a lot of travel up and down Superior."

That surprised me. I did not think of Superior as a well-used water highway prior to the voyageurs.

He assured me it was. "It was amazing how far people went in a canoe as part of their annual rounds," he said. "It was not uncommon to travel from Grand Portage to Sault Ste. Marie by canoe, for visiting or for trading. The Sault was at one time the cultural center for the Ojibway people."

*   *   *

From the front of the fort, facing the bay, we walked onto a long, wooden dock. Grand Portage Island was still wreathed in fog. I could see layers of fog descending from Hat Point.

"Is this where the voyageurs actually landed?" I asked.

"We don't know for certain," Cooper told me. "There's a place nearby that makes more sense."

"Show me," I said, and we walked along the front of the fort and crossed a small river. Not far away, I looked down at a beach. It was sandy, unlike the rocky areas in this bay.

"They would have run their canoes into the shallows," Cooper said. "The voyageurs would leap out to keep the canoes from grounding and damaging their bottoms. Then they'd unload."

He nodded his head in a northeasterly direction, and I could almost make out my boat's mast, bobbing at the marina, across the bay.

"Out there was their last landfall before Grand Portage. Beyond Hat Point, they'd clean themselves up, get ready for the final leg, and come around singing and racing to the beach. If they were the first brigade[2] in, the shores would be lined with people waiting for the news from Montreal, and firing guns. It would just have been a grand scene."

Not only the voyageurs arrived here, but so did the north men in their canoes. The rendezvous would begin — a big party — the only one of the year for some northmen.

Northman Karl Koster (above) wears a traditional long shirt at Grand Portage National Monument. In the rear is Grand Portage Island. Left, a sign beside the fur fort's dock warns "Danger, Extremely Cold Water." Below, on a fog-shrouded day, the author examines a replica voyageur canoe. Part of the old fur fort's wood stockade is shown on the right.

"But officials had to keep them away from the Montreal men, because they fought like cats and dogs," Cooper said.

I could imagine this grassy knoll filled with the brawling, rowdy canoe men.

Cooper explained, "The Montreal men were the lower end of the fur trade society. They were the greenhorns and were referred derisively as pork eaters by the northmen, as they had lard as part of their ratio. They were considered tenderfeet, even though the 1,200-mile paddle and a lot of brutal portages were no easy trip. Anyone who could do that would be no greenhorn by today's standards."

*   *   *

I left Cooper and explored the fort on my own. Walking around the southwest corner of the stockade, I came across a northman's encampment. It consisted of a shelter cloth attached to one side of the stockade, a small tent, and a fire site. Nearby was northman Karl Koster,

"Is that, er, a dress you're wearing?" I asked.

He was only momentarily taken aback. "Long shirt," the senior interpreter corrected me.

He explained that the long shirt, along with a breechclout and knee-high leggings, is preferable to traditional men's trousers. "You go through the woods a lot better."

In his work as a winterer in the northwest, Karl had done a lot of paddling in canoes and portaging though the woods. "The voyageurs paddled 40 to 60 strokes a minute," he said, handing me a paddle. "And they paddled 12 to 18 hours a day.

I hefted it, surprised that it was so lightweight and small. It was hand-carved out of lightweight cedar — a wood of which my own boat was made — and was small, allowing for a fast pace. Karl explained, "A wider paddle and you're going to get more resistance and give you a little more upper body wear."

The Montreal birch-bark canoe could be upward of 40 feet in length and carry a whopping 4 to 5 tons. The voyageurs ended up floating only six inches above the water. "You don't need a long paddle," Karl said.

"Even when you get 10 strong guys in a loaded canoe, you

can hardly move from a standing stop," he said. "The whole thing is momentum."

He demonstrated the beginning strokes, slow, little chops, then gradually increasing in length and power. "When she really gets kicking, you don't stop. You keep the momentum going."

"Mon ami," he said, appreciatively holding up his paddle. "Everyone knows of the voyageur's love of paddles. You even sleep with it."

They paddled long, hard hours in fragile birch-bark canoes, trying not to let Superior's storms stop them.[3] "Most were just farm boys out for the adventure and the scenery. It wasn't the pay that kept them coming back."

*   *   *

Located outside the stockade, the canoe house was a handsome two-story wooden building with a large door facing the bay. It was here that the canoes could be built, or equally important, rebuilt.

Inside were birch-bark canoes of all sorts, large and small, including voyageurs' canoes. I also found a pack of the type that a voyageur would carry. I tried to heft just one. I could hardly lift it a short distance from the ground.

That's because the pack weighed 90 pounds. Each pack contained 60 to 65 beaver pelts, and the voyageurs were expected to carry these on portages.

"They weren't considered much of a man if they could not carry two of them on their backs," Joyce Blanton, an interpreter, told me.

I knew voyageurs boasted about how many they could carry, but I could hardly imagine a voyageur carrying more than one in moccasin feet along a rough, woodland trail from lake to lake.

"There were three things a voyageur had to be: they could be 5 foot 6 inches to 5 foot 8 inches tall; it was a requirement that they not be able to swim; and another requirement that they had to know how to sing."

She explained that they had to sing to keep time and they

could not be tall or else their legs would take up too much room in the canoe. They'd also weigh too much.

And certifying that they could not swim?

That way the company was certain that if a canoe tipped over, the voyageurs wouldn't swim to shore — and refuse to come back.

But in the old days, many boys grew up wanting to be a voyageur.

"It's what they lived for, was to be a voyageur," she said.[4]

Chapter Six

THE BATTLE
OF THE
GRAMPA WOO

*The hollow winds begin to blow,
the clouds look black, the glass is low...
— Old sailor's saying*

LATE IN THE AFTERNOON as I returned to my boat, I took a long, hard look at nearby Grand Portage Island. It was still partially wreathed in fog, but I tried to imagine a white boat moored just off the island.

It wasn't there anymore — nor would it ever be.

It was at this little island about a mile across the bay from me that one of the most remarkable dramas of the Big Lake took place. It had shocked and saddened many sailors, including myself.

I had met the skipper and heard him tell the tragic story. His voice could not help betray emotion as he recalled the loss of his beautiful, 110-foot long aluminum vessel, the *Grampa Woo*[1] and the unusual chain of events leading up to the tragedy.

Luck had not been with the her. She had finished her season here on the North Shore and the skipper and crew had worked hard preparing her for a trip south to the Caribbean. The *Grampa Woo* was to have been off for a winter of fun down south.

She never made it.

* * *

It had all begun in the pre-dawn darkness of October 30, 1996, when Captain Dana Kollars had awakened with an uneasy premonition. Something bad was about to happen.

It was late in the year to be on the lake — nearing the dreaded gales of November. Dana and the *Grampa Woo* should have headed south[2] long ago, but she was moored in Grand Portage Bay with bare shafts, waiting for new propellers.[3]

Outside his home in Beaver Bay, the wind was starting to moan. Still half asleep and fighting off traces of exhaustion, he drove north on Hwy. 61. In the headlight's glare, fall leaves skittered nervously across the road; gusts of wind rocked his car and howled about.

Out on the lake, black hills were forming, topped with streaks of white. That meant an onshore wind — a bad one.

A weather system had moved in early. The barometer was falling to its lowest point in the history of the area.

Dana pushed the speeding car harder. His beloved *Grampa Woo* could be in trouble.

* * *

By 7:30 a.m., in the grim light of daybreak, Dana stood shivering on the end of the dock at Voyageur's Marina. Waves chopped at the pier; spray was driven horizontal by the wind.

Less than a mile away at her mooring off Grand Portage

Island, the *Grampa Woo* rode the gusts with aplomb, her sleek bow cocked bravely to windward. The *Woo* was holding steady at her 4,000-pound mooring.[4]

The ship's inflatable Zodiac was at the dock, so Dana told deck hand Robin Sivill to gas up its 35-h.p. outboard engine. Satisfied everything was still under control, he strolled off the dock to talk with Kek Melby, owner and operator of Voyageur's Marina.

"Captain," the deck hand yelled, running up to him. "*Grampa Woo* is moving."

"She's probably just shifting on her mooring," Dana responded. "Don't worry about it."

"She's moving!" the deck hand insisted.

When they arrived at the dock, the wind had increased and was blowing straight out of the west.[5] Half-filled, 55-gallon oil drums were being shoved off the pier.

As Dana squinted into the wind, the *Woo* slipped 50 feet.

Hurriedly, they threw the lines off the inflatable, gunned the engine, and headed out into the shallow bay to get to the *Woo*. The knife-like wind was on their starboard beam; the bay was alive now with three-foot-high waves. The speeding Zodiac took stringing spray aboard, dousing Dana and Robin, who were dressed in light jackets.

Halfway to the *Woo*, the outboard started to sputter and to miss.

If the engine stalled or quit, they'd be swept out the harbor's entryway into the raging lake without a radio or the proper clothing.[6] As the engine faltered, the inflatable bumped alongside the *Woo*, and the two clambered on board.

"That felt real good," Dana recalled. "It felt good to be on a nice, big ship."

Onboard, they fired up the engines. Although the *Woo* had no propellers, the power gave them the ship's electronics, including depth sounder, knot meter, global positioning system (GPS) and the all-important VHF— their radio lifeline.

They threw the ship's 80-pound Danforth overboard as well as another, smaller anchor, and increased the scope on the mooring. On the bow, they could see the anchors and the moor-ing line grow taut — and hold.

But the *Woo* had slipped 300 yards into 38 feet of water. With 200 feet of line out, they did not have enough scope on the anchors or the mooring to hold.

"And I knew that," Dana recalled later. "I knew that my other hope was that the second anchor would hold, and we would be able to increase the scope on that."

A wall of wind hit, and they could feel the *Grampa Woo* break loose. Dragging its heavy mooring and two large anchors across the bottom, the *Woo* headed through the harbor and out into the deep waters[7] of Superior. The seas had built alarming-ly.

Desperately, they threw out a sea anchor and the parachute-like device held the bow into the wind. In the pilot house, Dana checked the GPS and did some quick calculations. The *Woo* was moving backward at 4 1/2 knots (about 5 miles an hour) under wind power alone and was heading toward the reefs of Isle Royale.

They'd hit in several hours.

On the VHF radio, Dana put in a distress call to Kek at Voyageur's Marina, alerting him that they had blown out to sea. Kek told them he'd launch his 28-foot boat. It was a brave offer.

"You should stay," Dana advised him. "The seas are too high and the wind is too strong. You'll accomplish nothing except endangering your own life."

But there was no other boat at Grand Portage that could help. The *Woo* was not in Canadian waters and the nearest U.S. Coast Guard station with a boat big enough was in Duluth, Minnesota— more than 150 miles away, an eternity in these seas.

*   *   *.

In the distance, about eight to ten miles away, Dana saw an ore boat plowing through the heavy seas. She was the 1,000-foot-long *Walter J. McCarthy*, out of Duluth.

Dana, a retired U.S. Army officer who had once trained for

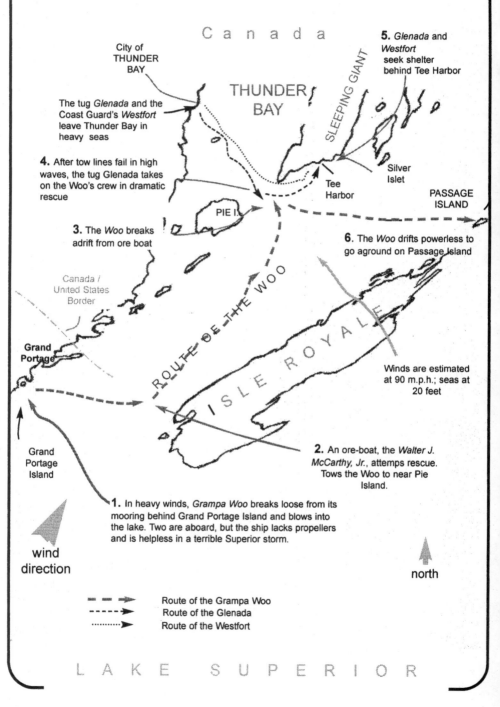

LAST VOYAGE OF THE *GRAMPA WOO*

Canada

City of
THUNDER
BAY

THUNDER
BAY

5. *Glenada* and
Westfort
seek shelter
behind Tee Harbor

SLEEPING GIANT

The tug *Glenada* and the
Coast Guard's *Westfort*
leave Thunder Bay in
heavy seas

Silver
Islet

Tee
Harbor

PASSAGE
ISLAND

4. After tow lines fail in high
waves, the tug Glenada takes
on the Woo's crew in dramatic
rescue

PIE I.

3. The *Woo* breaks
adrift from ore boat

6. The *Woo* drifts powerless to
go aground on Passage Island

Canada /
United States
Border

ROUTE OF THE WOO

Grand
Portage

Winds are estimated
at 90 m.p.h.; seas at
20 feet

ISLE ROYALE

Grand
Portage
Island

2. An ore-boat, the *Walter J.
McCarthy, Jr.*, attemps rescue.
Tows the Woo to near Pie
Island.

1. In heavy winds, *Grampa Woo* breaks loose from its
mooring behind Grand Portage Island and blows into
the lake. Two are aboard, but the ship lacks propellers
and is helpless in a terrible Superior storm.

wind
direction

north

— — — ➤ Route of the Grampa Woo
- - - - ➤ Route of the Glenada
· · · · · ➤ Route of the Westfort

LAKE   SUPERIOR

the priesthood, said later: "You know, there are times when you think everything is gone, and then God blesses you."

When Dana hailed the ore boat on the VHF, she altered course toward the drifting *Woo*. In the heavy seas, maneuvering the big ore boat was difficult, but on the second pass, the *McCarthy* was able to put her mass between the high seas and the *Woo*.[8]

"We felt a little bit like the duckling up against the hen and it was a comforting feeling," Dana recalled later.

The *McCarthy* sent down a three-inch thick cable. By the time they had secured the tow line to the *Woo*, the smaller boat had slipped to the stern of the *McCarthy* and the *Woo* pitched and pounded, on ten-foot bobs.

As Dana later recalled: "I'm a happy man. I've got a nice tow line, tucked in behind the stern of a great, beautiful thousand-foot ore boat, and headed for Thunder Bay, Canada."

Once the *Woo* got the tow line, Dana and Robin tried to retrieve the anchors still dragging in the water. But they discovered the lines were frozen. Their only option to clear the water was to cut them.

Half frozen themselves, they made their way back to the *Woo's* pilot house. The rolling and bumping between the ships had battered the *Woo's* side and tore up her bowsprit, but the captain and crew were secure in their ship.

"Of course, we had heavy seas, but as long as I could see that the tow line was taut, I was happy," Dana recalled.

*   *   *

As darkness started to fall, the storm grew worse. A snowstorm swirled about, hampering visibility. They passed the international border and were in Canadian waters, nearing the line of islands that guarded the stormy entrance to Thunder Bay.

On his cell phone, Dana called Thunder Bay Marine Services, Ltd., to have a tugboat meet the *Woo* by Pie Island, "and tow us into the marina, and tuck us into bed in a nice dock."

He also called the Thunder Bay Coast Guard, which said it

would come out and render assistance, if it possibly could.

Dana felt he had things reasonably in hand. He was under tow, he had a tug coming out to finish the voyage, and the Coast Guard was standing by.

He took time to call and reassure his wife, ChunAe, who was frightfully worried, and to talk to his son in Duluth, who had heard about the accident on television.

Abruptly, the *Woo's* motion changed. She lost speed.

Putting down his cell phone, Dana peered out the partially iced-over pilot house window and saw new trouble. After being stretched in hammering seas and frayed against the broken bowsprit, the three-inch towline had snapped.

The helpless *Woo* was drifting without power.

Dana could only stare helplessly into the growing darkness to see the thousand footer's ten-story structure grow smaller and smaller in the distance.

In 20-foot seas, they were alone once more.

Time and options were running out for the *Grampa Woo.*[9] She could drift in the heavy seas, until a rogue caught her beam to[10] and pulled them down, or she could slam up against the sharp reefs and rocky shoreline of Isle Royale.

It was dark. Snow was coming down hard and heavy ice was forming on deck.

*   *   *

The Canadian Coast Guard's patrol and rescue vessel, the 44-foot *Wesfort*, fought her way to the south, taking westerly winds on her starboard beam. It was a rough night on Thunder Bay — and they were encountering problems.

Chief Coxswain Bob King and crew Willie Trognitz and Inga Thorsteinson saw ice building up on their ship's mast and topsides.

The *Wesfort* was becoming top heavy, and if she iced up enough, she might not be able to right herself. She was not designed for these seas or this kind of weather.

Captain Gerry Dawson, aboard the *Glenada,* also was having problems. The 76-foot tug was more suited for the harbor than the open waters. As she pushed her way across Thunder

Bay's treacherous, reef-strewn waters, her low stern was awash with waves and her bow scooping up heavy water.

Below decks, Jack Olson, a four-decade veteran of Superior, was manning the engine room despite diesel fumes and the vessel's pitching and rolling. For the first time in his life, he was becoming seasick.

At 7 p.m., the *Glenada* reached the northeast tip of Pie Island and waited in the storm-tossed darkness. After about a half an hour, through swirls of snow, Gerry could barely make out the lights of the big ore boat, making its turn into Thunder Bay.

Off the *McCarthy's* stern, the lights of the *Woo* came into view. Gerry stared in disbelief. The two dim lights were growing apart.

The distance between the *McCarthy* and the *Woo* was increasing.

The tow line had snapped. The *Woo* was adrift, beam to in the twenty-two foot seas of the notorious Thunder Cape.

The *Glenada* charged out to the rescue.

*   *   *

The *Wesfort* continued to fight its way to the *Woo*, with crew member Inga Thorsteinson at the helm. The Coast Guard vessel's decks, superstructure, and mast became so heavily coated with ice that she was rolling down to nearly 90 degrees, practically on her side.

She had a bad hesitation before she came back up — top-heavy and in trouble.

Onboard the tug *Glenada*, deck hand Jim Harding donned a survival suit and struggled out into the spray. Beneath his running shoes, the deck was thick with wet ice, the kind on which you can't stand. Everything was ice coated: railings, rigging and the wheel house. The windows were iced up.

Jim dropped to his hands and knees and crawled forward to the towing lines. But he couldn't uncoil a single one.

All were frozen to the deck.

*   *   *

Dana saw the *Glenada*, ice covered and fighting the beam

seas, come into range — and pass him by.

She circled around several times, but never came close enough for a rescue attempt.

The crew of the tug kept searching but couldn't find a towing line it could use. All were frozen.

The *Woo* had a large spool of line sheltered inside the main salon. It was a three-fourths-inch diameter polypropylene line, the kind that floats.

Dana and Robin dragged it onto the ice-covered bow, and after the tug made three more passes, they tossed it in the churning water. It floated it downwind. On the *Glenada*, Jim caught the line, pulled it up to the bit and secured it.

But the stormy seas soon parted the line. The *Woo* was adrift again.

*   *   *

With the *Glenada's* wheelhouse completely iced over, Gerry's only vision was through a three-inch hole blasted open with a defroster. He peered about, but couldn't see his deck hand.

He grew worried. If Jim slipped into the high seas, he would have little chance of survival.

Unknown to the captain, Jim was just outside the wheelhouse, hanging on to the icy tow bollards, his legs afloat in the cascading seas on deck.

When the *Glenada* began to turn, Jim felt the position of wind and the waves change. He pulled himself along a hand rail to the wheel house, and reaching up with his wedding ring, tapped the glass.

Hearing the tapping, Gerry saw a hand waving outside the defrosted hole. He yanked open the pilot house door.

Jim Harding, half frozen and rimmed with spray ice, tumbled in.

*   *   *

Winds clocked out of the west at 90 miles an hour, and the seas were the worst they had been.

The *Glenada* carved through the waves, her decks constantly awash, her topsides continuing to ice up. At a little past 7 p.m., Gerry spun the wheel, and the *Glenada* turned around for one final — and desperate —attempt.

In the 22-foot seas, Gerry took a bearing through his peep hole, aimed his tugboat's massive bow at the *Woo*, and gave her power.

The *Glenada's* bow shoved against the *Woo's* stern hard enough to push in the aft deck railings. The two boats slammed together.[11]

On the *Woo's* deck, Dana and Robin balanced themselves on the bouncing rail. Above them, the *Glenada's* bow lunged up and down.

Timing the tug's motions, Dana jumped. On the *Glenada's* bow, Jim Harding reached down and pulled Dana, and then Robin, onboard.

"The deck was completely iced," Dana recalled. "We slid on board and as we slipped down past the wheelhouse door, we grabbed the door, and crawled in."

The *Grampa Woo* was now alone and adrift.

*   *   *

The *Glenada* and the *Wesfort* fought their way eastward, past the giant Thunder Cape, and swung into the protection of a low, flat island.

Without bothering to anchor, Gerry ran the *Glenada's* bow directly onto Tee Harbor's gravel beach. A short while later, the Canadian Coast Guard vessel came alongside.

In a secure harbor[12], but with both engines running, they waited out the storm. When the lake calmed enough, they sailed back to Thunder Bay. The city gave them a hearty welcome and lavished praise on the heroic work of the crew of the tug and the Coast Guard vessel.[13]

But what had become of the *Woo?*

*   *   *

Days later, the Coast Guard took Dana out to see his beloved ship. She had gone ashore on the rocks to the north and west of Passage Island, off Isle Royale.

"Just 400 yards, just 400 yards to the south, and *Grampa Woo* would have missed Passage Island," Dana said. "She would have been afloat the next day or two. We could have gone out and taken her back ashore."

From the sea, she looked salvageable, as though she just needed a tow off the rocks. But a closer inspection showed that she was crumpled up on her side and impaled on the rocks, her port side ripped open.

A few days later, another storm finished the job.

The once proud ship was in pieces, battered and stripped bare as she lay on the bottom. Half-inch aluminum was ripped as if it were paper. Heavy diesels had been ripped from the vessel, and everything on them was torn off: pumps, valve covers, and belts.

The largest single piece, the wheelhouse, was carried 150 feet away from the rest of the wreck. It was nearly intact, sitting upright on bottom as if it were waiting for its captain to come aboard and to sail away.

*   *   *

The end of the *Grampa Woo* had followed an unbelievable sequence of mishaps and bad luck.

Had Dana not removed the propellers when he did, the ship could have maneuvered under power against the blast of the wind. Had the wheels arrived when originally scheduled, the *Woo* would have been on her way south.

Had the wind not blown from the west, the *Woo* would not have been carried out of the harbor. Had the mooring held, or her anchors dug in, she would still be safe.

Had the tow line off the *McCarthy* not chafed through, the ore boat would have towed the *Woo* safely inside the protection of Thunder Bay's breakwaters.

Had the tow lines from the tug, *Glenada*, not been frozen to the deck, the *Woo* would also have survived a wild trip up Thunder Bay.

Had her final course been just one degree different, she would have blown clear of Passage Island, sailed through the straight, and merely drifted at sea until Captain Dana could tow her back to safety.

It was an overwhelming tragedy, a series of events that ultimately went wrong —one by one. Everything that could have been done was. Everything that was done failed.

The Big Lake had claimed yet another victim.

* * *

Several days after wreck of the *Grampa Woo*, ChunAe received a telephone call from the shipping company telling her that they had a large package addressed to her.

It was COD for $4,200 — the three propellers, ready at last.

The shipper wanted to know when to deliver them.

She was able to handle that call with some briskness.

* * *

It was a trip of more than 2,000 miles to bring the new boat from the Gulf of Mexico, up the rivers and waterways linking the middle of the continent,[14] and across Superior — back to their beloved North Shore.

But ChunAe, Captain Dana, and Robin Sivill were happy. Like the *Woo* before her, the *Grampa Woo III* was a heavy-weather boat designed to service offshore oil rigs. She was slightly longer at 115 feet, but also aluminum hulled and powered by three big diesel engines. With an enclosed dining area, private suites, and lots of seating, the beautiful ship would also go into service along the North Shore.

In the morning light, Dana slowed the powerful engines as he neared the four-mile gap between Isle Royale and Passage Island. The white ship followed the rocky coastline 400 feet and paused offshore, engines beating.

Beyond them, in pieces on the rocks and underwater, lay the remains of the original *Grampa Woo*.

It was ChunAe's first visit to the wreck site. With tears in her eyes, she bowed her head slightly and dropped a single, white flower into the water.

Then they sailed slowly away.

* * *

The final chapter in the saga of the *Grampa Woo* came when the U.S. National Park Service demanded removal of the wreck from the isolated park island.

Though Isle Royale has ten major wrecks underwater, the

wreck of the *Woo* fell under "dumping of trash, debris, and those sorts of things," according to the park's chief ranger, who was quoted as saying that federal laws demanded the boat's removal.

All traces of the wreck had to be removed to a depth of 130 feet.

It was fitting that the last remains of the *Grampa Woo* were removed by the captain who did so much to save its crew.

Captain Gerry Dawson sailed his tug with three barges over to Passage Island, and with the help of divers, pulled the last pieces of the *Woo* from the water.

Her 45 tons of wreckage were sold for scrap metal.

Part Two

THE GREEN STORM

The prudent sailor,
Before the sails be spread,
Searches the heavens
For a sign ahead.
—Weather saying

Waiting for the fog to lift on the lake, the author readies *Persistence*

Chapter Seven

SAIL PLAN

Fortune favors the audacious.
—Erasmus

TODAY WAS SATURDAY, July 3. I'd been at Grand Portage since Thursday, held back by high winds, fog, and unsettled weather. It looked like tomorrow might be just the day for which I was looking.

The weather forecast called for the 4th of July to be warm and humid, with a high of near 85 — the hottest day of the year so far.

That made me happy. I snapped off my radio and checked the thermometer inside the cabin: only 54 degrees. I felt the chill of the floor boards even through my heavy, wool socks.

I dressed in my polar fleece and walked up the dock, heading for Voyageur's Marina. Nearby was the 65-foot aluminum hulled excursion boat, the *Voyageur II*, which made regular runs to Isle Royale. On the speaker, the skipper was advising passengers there'd be a bumpy voyage today and that if they got sick they should go to the fantail.

"The worse place is the heads," he said ominously. He closed with a bit of north woods humor: "If you have any questions, we'll try to answer them. If we don't know, we'll try to make something up."

A little humor always lightens my day.

As the *Voyageur* left the dock, I glanced toward the awaiting lake. In the edges of the heavy fog, the sea was running from the day before in what is known as a dead roll. It was a motion that made people seasick.

But the sun was out and shining. And the forecast burned in my brain.

"I think I'll shove off tomorrow," I said to Sue Johnson at Voyageur's Marina. I settled down with a cup of coffee, half-listening to the noise of the marina's radio.

I added, "The forecast sounds good."

Sue shook her head. "We're having goofy weather this year," she said.

I listened closely.

"The wind is generally out of the west, but this year it's been northeast, and it blows day and night. Normally, it doesn't start blowing until 9 to 10 o'clock in the morning. Then it lays off at sunset. Not this year. It's been *goofy*." She placed special emphasis on the last word.

"The forecast is for thunderstorms tonight," I said. "It's supposed to clear on Sunday."

"Nice day on Sunday?"

"That's what they say. And that's when I'll take off for Canada."

She nodded thoughtfully, as if she had reservations about the forecast. I should have paid more attention.

*   *   *

Throughout the day, I worked to get my boat ready for tomorrow's shove off. I'd leave early, I decided — no sense in wasting the hottest day of the year.

I had tried unsuccessfully to get the Canadian weather forecast, but I couldn't receive the transmission. Something was blocking the radio waves — maybe the hills.

The darkness descended early and the harbor became eerily quiet, framed with the tree-shrouded hills. Across the waters, the old fur fort receded into the night. On the lake, the fog covered all.

At about 10 p.m., I checked my barometer. It read 30.32, showing Fair. I turned on the weather forecast. It reassured me tomorrow would be hot — the hottest day of the year. There would be clouds later.

In my *Boat Log & Record*, I wrote: "Good to go!"

I punched coordinates into my GPS unit. It would be a perfect day to sail north. I'd cross over the Canadian border to one of the small islands guarding the entrance to Thunder Bay. This would be the first leg of my trip.

Warm tomorrow! I held that thought in my mind as I slipped early into my sleeping bag. Tonight it was so chill I could see my breath.

Heck of a July night, I thought. I was dressed in a polar fleece sweat suit, long underwear, a wool cap and wool socks.

I fell asleep, rocked by my boat, the water gurgling not far from my head, and thinking pleasant thoughts about getting started.

*   *   *

I awakened at midnight to a terrible crashing noise and booming. The boat vibrated with the explosions.

Jumping up, I peered anxiously out my port light. The sky was alive with streaks of lightning, crackling across the sky, jaggedly illuminating the harbor.

An electrical storm had come up suddenly. It had not been forecast.

Goofy weather. Again.

Maybe the storm was just clearing the air, I rationalized.

I settled back in my bunk, pulling my cap over my ears to muffle the storm's noise. Tomorrow would be the 4th of July.

A great day — just like the forecast said.

Chapter Eight

NO PLACE TO RUN,
NO PLACE TO HIDE

*There is but a plank
Between a sailor and eternity.
— Edward Gibbon*

SUNDAY MORNING, THE 4TH OF JULY — I shivered and looked out my portlight. I wasn't going anywhere, not in this pea-soup fog. The weird electrical storm of the night before hadn't cleaned up the atmosphere at all.

Where was the bright, sunny, hot July 4th that had been forecast? [1]

Discouraged, I stalked off the dock to see Sue and Kek at the marina, and to mooch some of their coffee.

"It'll burn off. You'll be OK." They seemed unconcerned by the fog.

After a cup of coffee, I walked back to the dock and looked around the harbor. Grand Portage Island was beginning to clear, its dark shape visible, though the fog wrapped around it heavily. Across the bay, the old fur fort was starting to emerge. I could see the sharp points of its stockade.

But outside of the harbor, the fog hung like a thick gray blanket. Cold. Sinister.

I returned to my boat to get ready. Inside the cabin, I pulled everything that had any weight or bulk² out of the stern and the stem and secured it alongside the centerboard case. I clambered topside to take off the ties to the jib furler and to remove the mainsail cover. I checked the mainsail; it was held securely in place on the boom with elastic shock chord.

I snapped my GPS into its holder and crossed my fingers. This would be the first time I'd actually use my new GPS for open water navigation.

It was supposed to be the hottest day of the year, but I wore cotton long johns under a pair of heavy sweatpants, an arctic pile pullover, and a pile-lined nylon boating jacket. On my feet, I had wool socks and boating mocs.

Superior was not to be trusted, no matter what the forecast said.

*   *   *

Patchy fog lay outside the harbor as I nosed my way into the lake. I was crouched in my inside steering position, my nose about a foot from the plastic windshield. Though it was warmer in here than in the open cockpit, I could still feel the fog's clammy, cold touch.

"Security, security," I called out on my VHF to alert any vessels of my position. I didn't get an answer. Not too many boats would be dumb enough to be out in this pea-soup fog.

The big lake was as cold as a snowstorm, eerie in its formlessness and silence. The only sound was the gurgling of the water passing the hull and the muted growl of the outboard engine.

I was glad I had worn the warm clothing or I'd be shivering by now.

Fog or no fog, we were on our way at last.

*   *   *

Slowly, the morning brightened. I moved back into the cockpit, my hand firmly gripping the tiller.

Below me, the waters of the icy lake glistened down far into its depths. Gliding through the easy swells, we seemed to be flying upon translucent air. We were aloft on the world's greatest freshwater lake.

Beautiful, small islands began to glisten in the weak sunlight, while further out on the lake, the fog wreathed ethereally.

But on the hazy, high bluffs of the headland, the fog hadn't lifted. Its cap of blue-gray didn't look quite right.

I moved my head around, feeling for a breeze on my face. There was nothing worthwhile; this was an eerie day. There was a peculiar heaviness to the air I could not explain.

As I neared Victoria Island, I picked up my mike and called the Thunder Bay Coast Guard. I was now across the International Boundary, in Canadian waters.

I filed my Sail Plan, telling them where I was, my course heading, and where I was going. I gave them an estimated time of arrival (ETA) of 2:30 p.m. at Thompson Cove,[3] one of the outermost islands guarding the mouth of Thunder Bay.

I shrugged. I'd do that easy.

Something made me look over my left shoulder. Behind me, the crown of dark, bluish fog was sweeping off the land and heading out to sea. It looked like another fog bank, or at worst, a rain cloud. Although it had grown bigger and darker, it was still a long way off.

But it definitely was heading in my direction.

I turned up my engine to half throttle, and with a healthy snarl, *Persistence* began moving faster.

We'd tuck into the cove on Thompson Island long before anything hit us.

*   *   *

The sky grew overcast, then dark and gray. The water turned the color of lead, and the air had a tomb-like chill.

Not good at all, I decided, so I moved back into my inside steering position and closed the flap behind me. If it rained, I'd be warm and dry inside my dodger.

Ahead lay Spar Island, after that, a line of reefs running northeast to Thompson Island, a little more than five miles away.

Where was the cove? I grabbed my cruising guidebook and my chart and began studying them. It'd be easy. All I had to do was cruise along the south side of Thompson until I came to a cove not far from the island's eastern tip.

The VHF came to life sounding a harsh, alternating tone, a warning of some kind. I did not know what it was, but I could make out "dangerous weather."

Above the static a few minutes later came the dread words, *"Mayday! mayday!"*

Somewhere north of me, a sailboat had capsized. People were struggling in the water. What was going on?

The sky grew darker. I felt very lonesome out here.

*   *   *

The first drops of rain felt like little bombs on my canvas dodger. They were cold and heavy, followed by gusts of wind that made my boat shake. I felt the mast heel a little, then recover.

I wasn't too worried. There are always a few gusts when some heavy weather hits, but these spend themselves quickly.

But the wind came from the northwest, out of the fog area, rushing down from the hills.

Something was back there.[4] The wind was hitting my boat on its all-too-vulnerable portside beam.

I punched in a new course and the Autohelm hummed, directing the tiller to steer us downwind. I'd present my transom directly toward the wind — a classic storm tactic. A few minutes of this, the gusts would subside, and I'd resume course.

Suddenly, a wall of wind, powerful and unrelenting,

screamed at me. It caught us in its grip and threw us forward, skittering, faster and faster, and suddenly we stopped, pitching down, beam to the onrushing windstorm.

I fell sideways, hard. From below came a crash. I saw my alarm clock and other gear fly from one side of the boat to another. Some of it landed atop me. Pain stabbed my right side, and I realized I was lying on my back, looking up..

The cold waters of Superior rushed up to fill the starboard portlight with an evil green color. Part of the cabin was underwater.

"*This is it*," my brain warned. "*We're going over.*"

The boat teetered dangerously.

The wind screamed like a banshee. I saw water slosh up through the open centerboard case.

I could feel an icy chill in my heart. We were turning over, slowly, oh so slowly.

I braced myself. We were not coming back up.

From behind me the auto pilot clacked noisily, over as far as it could go, and unable to make a course change. The engine was howling, the prop out of the water.

We were caught in the teeth of the storm. Out of control.

If the wind could get a grip on the high side of my hull, it could shove my boat over. We'd capsize all the way, rolling upside down, mast down, bottom up.

She'd never come up from that.

I'd be underneath.

My survival suit was under the portside bunk. No time to get to it. No time to do anything.

Somehow, I pulled myself up and tore out of the dodger, grabbing the high, windward lifelines. Rain pelted my face as I faced my enemy.

The lake was cold and gray, its surface scoured flat by the terrible wind. Long contrails of mist whipped across the water like icy whips.

I turned in time to see four heavy rubber fenders tear away from the cockpit and fly away.[5]

My boat balanced on its side, reeling with every gust. The

mast spreader dipped into the water, then rose a little unsteadily.

Hand over hand, I crawled back to the transom. I jammed my thumb down on the autopilot's red button, turning it off. My hand closed in a death grip on the tiller.

Another huge gust tore into us. I felt us go down farther.

No! I threw myself over the windward lifelines as far as I could, but the boat still was on its side and out of control. I could only hang on.

After what seemed like an eternity, we came upright with a mighty splash. The mast flew upward. The engine's racing stopped as the prop bit solid water. We picked up speed.

I jammed the tiller over, heading farther off the wind. Now we were taking the wild gusts on the transom instead of our vulnerable beam.

But we were rapidly heading away from the islands — and any chance of shelter — deeper into the raging lake.

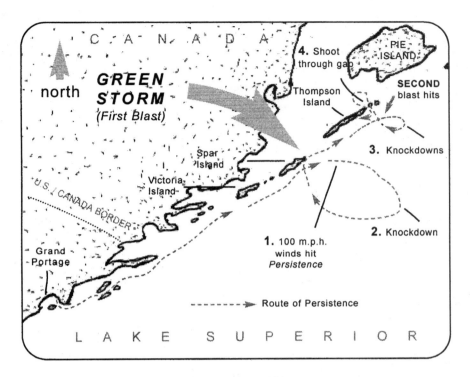

Chapter Nine

FIGHT TO
THE ISLAND

Oh, hear us when we cry to thee,
For those in peril on the sea.
—William Whiting

THE ENGINE POPPED OUT of the water, racing madly. I leaned out, adding my weight to the windward side, and we fought our way upright with me hanging on for dear life.

The boat was unstable, like a teeter totter — heading out deeper into the lake.

The wind slammed into us again. Down went the mast, up came the water, and out I went, leaning over the edge. It occurred over and over again, in a maddening battle of knockdowns.

I was shivering uncontrollably. The billed cap I had pulled down low on my forehead kept some of the driving rain off, but my glasses were misted with water. I couldn't see too well.

I was in a world of hurt. I had no place to run to, no place to hide, and nobody to help me.

Another violent gust flattened us. As the boat laid over this time, to my horror, I heard a "ping" noise.

Something had snapped.[1]

I saw the mainsail come loose from its shock chords. The wind's fingers began to shove it up the mast. The big sail reared a third of the way up, flapping, rattling, and catching the wind.

My heart pounded.

The boat was on the edge of capsizing. What would happen with some sail up?

I could not leave the tiller. The only answer was to run on with the wind, deeper into the lake, until something broke or the wind let up a little.

I clenched my teeth and tightened my grip on the tiller. I would not give up.

*   *   *

Finally, I sensed the wind letting up a little; at least the insane gusts were not shoving us over quite so far.

"Do it!" I steeled myself. Timing the gusts, I shoved the tiller over hard — and I hung on.

Persistence did a dangerous dip to leeward, hung down on her rail for a moment — and finally turned.

We were facing the wind. The sail rattled on the mast, and the boat felt terribly unstable underneath me.

One hand on the tiller, I reached back and gave the outboard full throttle and locked it there.

Power. I simply had to have more power in the teeth of the storm. The engine would just have to take it.

The little Nissan bellowed and dug in. The boat bounced up and down, careening sideways. Sometimes the prop was in the water; sometimes it was out. The engine revved unmercifully and screamed.

We were gaining.

Through my rain-soaked glasses, I could make out an island ahead. How could this be?

I had already passed Spar Island and had been abeam of the rock-shoals leading to Thompson.

Where was I?

*   *   *

It was a low, wind-swept rock. Not much shelter, it seemed to me, but as I came closer, I found that the bluffs were higher than I realized.

Where were the reefs? I could only hope that this side of the island was bold and deep up to its shoreline.

As I came into its lee, I throttled down. The wind was still howling, but the island was deflecting the main blasts.

To my starboard lay some rocky pinnacles, now awash in the storm. In the distance, I could make out a larger island. I must have done a complete loop in the storm and doubled back to Spar Island.

Little comfort. There was no place for me to hide on this barren island.

My heart was pounding and my muscles were knotted tight. I was shivering uncontrollably and practically gasping in the cold rain as I shoved the tiller over and began to run alongside the sheltering island. Overhead, and out on the lake, the storm still raged.

I wiped my glasses with my fingers. Ahead lay a row of spectacular rocky pinnacles, slashed with waves and spray. They stretched from the northeastern edge of Spar out into the lake. In the distance, I could make out a gray headland.

It had to be Thompson Island.

I twisted the throttle, and we roared ahead. The boat again caught the brunt of the storm.Persistence staggered, her speed diminished, her rail dipping low into the water. Wind shrieked in the rigging, wrestling with the mast.

I edged out over my port side, my leg locked around the traveler beam, one arm around a winch. The tiller was in a death grip.

Small, rocky islets — spray everywhere — flew by. I was desperate to reach Thompson Cove.

I hoped my progress would not be interrupted by a reef.

I reached down for my chart and a cruising guidebook, which I had jammed to one side of the gas tank. Both were soaked; ink was running where I had marked my course. I dared not let the wind get these—-my only guides to where I wanted to go.

I glanced at my dodger, its back cover flapping wildly in the gusts. Above it the partly-raised sail rattled and tore at the mast, but it did not seem to be going any higher.

I wished I could move forward to grab my GPS unit, pro-grammed for the coordinates of Thompson cove. But I dared not leave my steering.

I'd just have to find the harbor — somehow.

I was headed for a small cove on a small island. How tough could that be? I'd just run alongside Thompson on the leeward side, far enough out to avoid any reefs, but close enough to see the cove.

I checked my watch. I told the Coast Guard I'd be in harbor in 45 minutes.

All I had to do was maintain course and spot the cove.

I'd have time to spare.

*   *   *

As we came under the lee of Thompson, the island shouldered the wind off me. I breathed a sigh of relief and began watching the shoreline.

I slipped past a large cove — there was no entrance — then rapidly approached the end of the island.

If I ran all the way to the tip of Thompson, I'd have to come across the entry to the cove. Easy.

I glanced my NOAA chart again. There was nothing officially designated as Thompson Cove. The name only appeared with a detail drawing in my cruising guide book. In the jouncing, rain-soaked cockpit, it was hard to read.

Scanning the shore, I saw a rocky cliff leading down to the water's edge, its crest topped with trees. Farther away, lashed by waves and spray, a small, round island stood its lonely sentinel.

Shivering in my cockpit, glasses blurred with rain and spray, I headed to the tip of the island.

*   *   *

Off in the distance, I saw a dark blue line etched on the water. It was moving — rushing toward me.

That much blue on the water meant only one thing: wind.

Tons of it.

With a howl, the wind raced across the channel between the islands. The storm had switched from the west, veering to catch me.

The lake wasn't done with me yet.

The first blasts shook my boat, screaming past my partly hoisted sail, grabbing it and making it hammer with a deadly resonance.

The tiller twisted in my hand as the boat bucked and took a dive to starboard.

We were back down on our side, cabin going partly under, mast spreaders dipping in the water. Icy waves climbed the side of my boat and splashed into the cockpit.

I leaned my weight out over the cockpit, but the boat simply couldn't stand up to this windstorm. She kept careening down at a terrifying angle, mast nearly underwater, as I wrestled with the useless tiller.

I cranked the throttle back up to maximum. With a deep snarl, the little engine leaped to full r.p.m.s. The boat smashed into the waves.

Where was the cove? I was shivering uncontrollably — wondering if I was courting hypothermia.

But all I could do was hang on — and pray.

We neared a dangerous place — a gap between the land and a small island. A wave tore at the rocks, flinging spray high into the air. As it raced on, I shuddered. A teeth of reefs lay just beneath the waves.

Beyond, a mile or so away, lay something green. Land — the island. And the cove.

Out of the stormy waters, another boat headed toward me. It shot the narrow gap, bouncing like a log in a mountain stream. It was a large sailboat, with a tall mast but no sail up, and running hard under power.

Why were they headed this way? I shook my head to clear it.

They had come from where I wanted to go.

Still, I persisted. As I fought my way upwind, they turned around the tip of the land, heading westerly. I lost sight of them.

I took a deep breath. Adrenalin surging, I charged the gap.

I had to make it to the island.

Suddenly, I lost control. In a heart-stopping moment, we careened dangerously toward the islet's foam-lashed reefs, black teeth showing ominously.

I swore, prayed, steered, and careened my weight. Finally, the boat came back up and obeyed me.

We circled back — to try again.

This time, I worked my way further east — behind the protection of the tiny islet, letting it take the blast of the waves and wind.

I braced myself and squeezed the throttle hard to be sure I

had every last ounce of power the engine could give me. We charged, picking up speed.

We bounced, careened, splashed — and suddenly, we were through the gap.

On the other side, I was awestruck at the size of the waves. My speeding bow speared into the first oncoming tower. The impact shook my boat.

The bow disappeared. The water kept coming over the cabin top — and hit me in the chest.

I groaned at the impact and the chill of the icy water.

We climbed the wave, teetering at the top. For the first time, I could see what lay ahead.

I was facing huge, square rollers — the worst waves I'd fought all day. There was a sea of them out there, all headed toward me.

Something was terribly wrong. Ahead lay not a cove, but another island. A very big island.

It finally came to me. My stomach lurched with despair.

That big, distinctive island ahead of me was none other than Pie Island. Somehow, we had overshot our destination.

I had made a mistake —- maybe a fatal error.

We could not live out here.

*   *   *

Desperately, I timed the waves, and on the back of one of the steep chargers, I turned the little boat around — and roared back to the dangerous gap.

We were flying now, nearly surfing the waves, almost out of control.

We were up on the crest, then down in the trough. Monsters reared behind me.

Ahead, the gap loomed, waves crashing on either side, the black teeth of reefs yawning.

We were through. I turned westward.

I tried to figure things out. The other sailboat had come through here and headed westward.

But where was it?

I was growing tired. My reactions were slowing; it was hard

to think. I was thoroughly doused in icy water, shivering uncontrollably, cold through almost to my body core.

I roared at full throttle back up Thompson Island. Rocky slopes rushed past me, close by my speeding boat. Beyond one crag, I saw something shining. Up high, above the trees.

I squinted, trying to clear my focus.

Unmistakably, they were sailboat masts — just the tops of them.

The water widened. On one side was a high outcrop of rock, and on the other, a spruce-covered hill.

And in between, still, blue water.

The cove! Blessed, beautiful Thompson Cove.

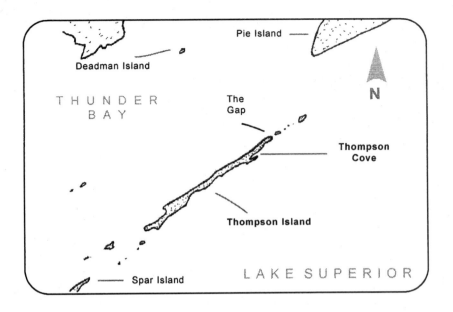

Chapter Ten

THE WELCOME ISLAND

Behold, now, another providence of God.
A ship comes into the harbor.
—William Bradford

I BLINKED SEVERAL TIMES and shakily arose in my cockpit. Ahead of me lay calm, blue water surrounded by steep slopes. The wind was gone — and I knew why.

I was in the island's cove, and — most important — off the lake. This welcome island was shouldering the blast. The sun was out, the world was Technicolor bright and summer again.

As I slipped into this sheltered natural harbor, I turned down the racing engine. Shivering in my wet clothing, I peered ahead through wet eyeglasses. Along the shoreline were five sailboats, including one with blue trim. I could see people rushing to the sides of the sailboats, pointing down at me.

"Can I come alongside?" I yelled. There was no space left

on the small dock, so I would need to tie up alongside another boat.

"Raft up here," answered a friendly Canadian.

"Got a line?" someone asked. I tossed him one.

"I lost all my fenders," I said. I needed them to raft up alongside a boat.

"No problems," someone said. "I've got an extra one," someone else shouted. "Here's another," another sailor added. They came up with four fenders and began helping tie them onto the boat.

I turned off my engine and looked up at my newly found friends. This was a most welcome island — and I had been most fortunate to land among some very fine people.

"*Persistence*," I heard my VHF boom urgently. "Calling the sailboat *Persistence*."

It was the Thunder Bay Coast Guard. Realization hit me. I was overdue on my ETA, and they were ready to initiate a search-and-rescue mission. I had not heard them calling when I was in the cockpit surrounded by all the noise of the storm and the engine.

I grabbed the mike and told them I was just tying up inside Thompson Cove and that I was off the lake. "Sorry," I finally blurted, by way of apology. "But I've been a little busy."

We signed off.

"A sauna's good after that sail," one Canadian boater solicitously called down to me. "It'll warm you right up."

I thanked the sailors, but went back down below. Tired and soaked to the bone, my first thought was to grab a towel and get into dry clothing.

I was confronted with chaos. Everything loose within the boat now was scattered in a mess everywhere. Priority one was to straighten up and check out the boat.

I began moving gear around, unfastening bags from beside the centerboard trunk. Cautiously, I checked below.

To my surprise, the bilge was filled with water. Normally, all that's down there is dust. Now I had a couple of inches in the deepest part of the bilge. Cans of soup and Dinty Moore stew were floating in it. Had I broken something? Had the hull sprung a leak?

Fears shot anew through my mind. Then I remembered all too vividly what had happened in the storm. When the boat went on its beam ends, I saw water gush through the open centerboard trunk.[1]

Another quick recollection: when I dashed out of the dodger, I had taken on rainwater through the open hatch. I remembered the unsecured cover flapping in the downpour.

Probably nothing to worry about, I thought, as I bailed out the water. I finished drying the bilge with a large boat sponge.

That would take care of the boat for now. I also had cleared a passage to the forward bunk. When I found my clothing duffel bag, I loaded my arms with clean clothing, a towel, and a dry pair of boat moccasins.

But when I exited the hatchway, I had trouble standing upright. The hours I had spent during the storm were taking their toll on my stressed back and leg muscles. A small pain throbbed in my right side, where I had fallen against the hatchway during the knockdown. My left ankle ached, the result of an old sprain.

All that paled in insignificance as I stood on dry land. It felt solid under my feet; the land did not rock. I pulled myself slowly upright and looked around.

Thompson Cove was not large, but a jewel of a natural harbor, set between heavily wooded ravines. A wooden walkway ran alongside the dock, cantilevered over the water from the steep, rocky cliffs. The walkway encircled a tree, dodged around a big rock, and snaked around a cliff, with wooden benches built in. It was like somebody's sculpture garden.

My clothing squished as I walked along a heavily wooded trail to the end of the cove. Nestled among trees was a modern-looking, A-frame wooden structure. Smoke lazed out of a chimney; beside the unpainted building was a pile of cut wood.

Letting my layers of sodden clothing fall off me, I entered the sauna. I was still shaking, and feeling blue-ish, but someone had stoked up the fire. I threw a dipperful of water on the hot stones and sat back to enjoy the steam. The heat permeated me and my body began to unwind. Stiff, aching muscles began to unkink, and a remarkable sense of well-being came over me.

Whoever built a sauna on this remote island certainly had good sense. I discovered there is nothing better after a long, cold sail than a hot sauna. I took my time warming up, instilled anew with the wonders of this remarkable and most welcome island.

Greatly refreshed, I clambered aboard my little sailboat. I hung my wet clothing and gear off the boom and the lifelines, where they flapped in the light breeze. The heat beamed down on me, making me perspire.

If there were strong winds out on the lake, I could not feel them here. I spent a few minutes just bobbing in my island paradise, so peaceful and calm.

Then I ducked below to further check out my boat. Nothing seemed damaged, except my alarm clock and my wristwatch. The clock had flown from one side of the cabin to another during the knockdown and had stopped. I checked the batteries and shook it; it only worked when it stood upright. My wristwatch had been torn from my wrist when I fell and I found it, missing a strap pin, on the floorboards.

I unfolded my soggy charts, and, along with my wet guidebook, set them out in the sun to dry out.

I realized I was moving slowly. It seemed incredible that only a short time ago I was shivering in my long johns and polar fleece.

And out there, fighting that incredible storm.

My mind kept coming back to what had happened only hours before. I'd survived a storm the likes of which I'd never encountered before — and hoped never to come across again.

But there was another survivor. I had seen him roaring through the wave-churned gap. He was here on the island with me.

*   *   *

I sauntered down the dock to a white sailboat with blue trim bobbing easily in the quiet cove. Mike Fabius, of Thunder Bay, was aboard his 33-foot CS sloop, *Easy Blue*.

We began chatting, and he told me he was not on the open waters of Superior when the storm erupted, but had been peacefully at anchor in a bay to the south of Pie Island. Onboard was his son, Alistair, and four of Alistair's high school friends.

"We could hear the rumbling in the background," Mike said. They had been ashore on the island and returned to the boat in time to see clouds blocking the hills. They pulled up their anchor, moved the boat to deeper water, and put down their 35-pound, plow-type anchor.

"The sky turned a bright green, with some sort of fluorescent in it," Mike told me. "I've never seen anything like it before."

Pie Island was directly to the north of Thompson. It was the island that I found myself mistakenly headed toward after I had shot through the gap. It was a high, bold island.

"I thought we were secure," the skipper said, "but we started dragging and the boat was twisting sideways."

"The winds were extreme. They actually rotated 90 degrees," he said.

I remembered all too well. "That was my impression, too," I said. "The wind came from two different directions."

Mike told me what happened next. The rain pounded down like pellets, and there was lightning everywhere. At the wheel, Mike sent Alistair and a teen-age friend forward, but in the high winds they couldn't get the anchor up. Mike turned his engine to full power to ease the strain.

But the hook was still dragging. The boat was being swept downwind.

"The boat was leaning at 45 degrees, and I was afraid the anchor line was going to snap," Mike said. "There was white spray moving horizontally several feet above the waves in 100-foot lengths, then pulling up like tails."

In between gusts, the boys somehow wrestled the hook up and the skipper turned the boat downwind.

"There wasn't a lot of choice," Mike said. "The waves were six to eight feet and coming from two directions."

"That must have been about when I saw you," I said. I remembered being surprised to see another boat out there in the storm.

"And we saw you, too. You were really moving, despite the waves."

I remembered that, as I fought for control on my own boat, I had watched them shoot the gap at the end of Thompson Island, with waves crashing on rocks on either side.

"We had made it through the gap before." Mike explained. He added thoughtfully, "The waves were fierce."

"Any idea of the wind speed?"

"I only thought to check my anemometer after the worst gusts were past," he said. "It read 72 knots (about 85 miles per hour)."

"I heard a mayday on the radio earlier," I said. "A sailboat capsized."

"I know them. They were headed back to Thunder Bay when their sailboat got caught."

I started to ask him what had happened, but I realized he wouldn't know. He'd been out in the islands, like me.

There were a lot of questions about the storm that were unanswered. Here on the island, I was only getting bits and pieces of the storm story.

"Must have been some gusts coming through," he added.

I nodded. These were the worst winds I had ever been out in.

"Some afternoon." He shook his head.

*   *   *

At about 6 p.m., shadows were falling along the harbor. I snapped on my VHF radio and called the Thunder Bay Coast Guard. "I'd like to make a long distance telephone call," I said.

It was a little miracle. Here I was, in my little sailboat on a remote island on Superior, about to talk to my wife by telephone. This was our prearranged meeting time.

"So," I said carefully, "how is your Fourth of July?"

"Good," Loris answered cheerfully, telling me how she and our son Will were getting ready to have a barbecue in the back yard. It was a hot, sultry day back in Shoreview.

"And how was your trip?" she inquired.

"I'm tied up in a wonderful, little island," I said. "Thompson Cove."

It was succinct, but true. We were broadcasting on a radio frequency that anyone could listen in on, so we had agreed to be careful in our choice of communications. I hoped I had arrived at the right balance between telling the truth and not getting her too worried about me and my boat. I did not want to cause her and Will pain. There'd be time for the details to come out later.

"There was a report of high winds up north," she said carefully. "Parts of Hwy. 61 were washed out."

"Oh," I said, trying to sound nonchalant. "I came across a storm on the way in. But we're fine."

*   *   *

A warm, gentle night fell early, and darkness came to the island. The only lights were those shining through the boat's portlights, and, on shore, a few hardy souls with flashlights returning from a visit to the ever-popular sauna.

I rummaged around my still-damp bilge and selected my fare for this evening's dining. It would be a can of stew, heated on my single-burner stove.

As I enjoyed my leisurely dinner, I thought about Loris and Will back home with their barbecue. I wished I could join them. I hoped they did not worry about me.

I ate out of the pan in which I had heated the stew, and then washed it. Dinner done, I crawled into my sleeping bag. It had been a long, eventful day, and I welcomed my warm and recuperative sack time.

I felt the boat move rhythmically in the water, and I began to synchronize myself with the slight movements. The water was just inches away from my head; I could hear it lapping gently against the wooden hull. It made a wonderful mantra that quickly lulled me to sleep.

Sometime during the night, I awoke shivering and chilled to the bone. I could not believe I could be this cold. I already had on long johns and heavy wool socks, but I pulled on a woolen hat, my polar fleece, and piled a fleece blanket over my sleeping bag.

Even under all these layers, it took a while before I started to warm up again.

I had just fallen asleep again when I was awakened by bright flashes. I heard a jarring noise. I jumped up and put on my glasses to look out the portlight. Lightning danced about the skies to the north, illuminating the island's rocky spires.

The electrical display was followed by a great gush of wind that slammed my little boat against its fenders, causing it to rock from side to side, groaning against the bigger boat to which I was rafted.

I wasn't too worried about the rafting, but I realized that my wet clothing hung from my cockpit lifelines and boom.

A torrent of rain fell as I threw open the dodger cover and I could feel the cold pellets slam down on my head and shoulders. I grabbed the sodden clothing and gear and I threw it below to the floorboards.

Shivering again, I closed the canvas cover and sat back, toweling off, listening to the rain thumping on my cabin.

I took stock. I'd been lucky. If the stuff hadn't been soaked and sodden, I'd have lost it in the winds.

I realized I'd have to be a lot smarter to survive on this lake.

I could only hope I'd learn in time.

In Thompson Cove, Jo Ann and Lynn Bradford relax aboard *Timothy Lee*

Chapter Eleven

LIFE ON A
SMALL ISLAND

There's a welcome sweet that awaits you
In the land where you would be.
— from a sea chantey

DROWSILY, I LIFTED THE FLAP on my dodger and poked my head out. It was 8 a.m. and a bright, sunny morning. There was no sign of the early morning thunderstorm.

"Hello, the little boat," came a fine Canadian voice from somewhere above me on the dock. "Are you all right?"

I cocked one eye open. "Yes, just fine," I said.

"Come over for some coffee," Gillian Rowe offered, and

moments later I had pulled on some outer clothes and made my way onto their large sailboat, *Capricorn II*, to enjoy coffee and home-made coffee cake.

"You might as well come in with us," she offered, her husband, John, nodding assent. "The weather's going to be rotten for the next five days. We'll find you space at the marina, and you can stay with us. We've got an extra bedroom."

It was a tempting offer: to sail into Thunder Bay[1] and put up my boat for a few days until the weather cleared. I glanced out a portlight; on the nearby hills of the island, fog lay like a cotton blanket.

She saw my concern. "That'll burn off," she said.

It wasn't the pea-soup fog that bothered me. Besides, I really liked this island.

"Thanks anyway," I said. "I might as well stick here for a while."

*   *   *

A little later that morning, *Capricorn* and the other Thunder Bay boats untied from the dock and motored off into the fog bank. I watched them go, one by one: *Easy Blue, Capricorn, Forever*, and *Rock Bottom*.

It was a little sad, seeing my Canadian friends leave, but they explained that the weekend was done, and they had to get back. These were their home cruising waters, and they'd pick their way through the fog just fine. Each had a GPS, and I saw one of the navigators punching in his waypoints. Even if he could not see in the fog, he could move from leg to leg to navigate the reef-strewn area of Thunder Bay.[2]

Only one other sailboat and I were left in the cove.

The radio forecast an unstable air mass over Ontario, with winds in the 30- to 40-kilometer-per-hour range, with waves of one to two meters (three to six feet). There was a warning to mariners in effect.

It seemed like a good day to keep my little boat here in the cove. Here, the morning was pleasant, with sunshine peeking through, illuminating the water. Above me to the north, fog encircled the peaks.

I decided to move my boat forward along the dock for a better position. I untied both dock lines, then walked forward, but I found myself unaccountably weary and had to stop to rest. My side hurt from where I had fallen, and my muscles were stiff. My knees groaned and creaked; my left ankle hurt.

I could pretty much ignore the pain, but the one thing I couldn't compensate for was that I lacked energy. I felt as if I were moving in slow-motion. I forced myself to think and act deliberately.

Move the hand, then step forward. Tug on the boat.

Tote that barge, lift that bale...

Slowly, I got my boat repositioned on the dock and tied it off. I opened the hatches and pulled sodden clothing out again to dry on the lifelines. I also pulled up the floorboards to let the bilge and my canned goods dry out.

Now came a matter that I had to get to. Yesterday, because my one outboard engine had failed to start, my departure was delayed by more than an hour. I frowned as I remembered; I had yanked repeatedly on its starting chord, checked connections, choked it, then unchoked it, and finally, even changed the brand new sparkplug. But nothing was working. It simply would not start.

Today, I decided to try again. I swung the outboard down into the water on its bracket, pumped up the pressure bulb, opened the choke, and yanked — hard. With a roar, the Mariner engine fired into life on the first pull and ran perfectly. Amazed, I let it run for a while to warm up, then turned it down to idle.

I snicked it into gear at the dock and tried forward and reverse; both worked perfectly. If it started now, it would start again if I should need it. I was back to two engines.

Why didn't it start yesterday? Maybe the previous night's monsoon-like rain got to it.

Maybe... Who knew?

"Would you like to stop by for dinner?" I looked up, turning off the engine.

It was the couple on board the *Timothy Lee*, a massive Baba

35 cutter, the other boat in the cove besides me. "We caught a fish, and it's too much for us to eat alone."

I was delighted to join Jo Ann and Lynn Bradford, from Duluth, Minnesota. They explained that Lynn usually tows a hook behind the sailboat, but this was the first time he'd ever caught a fish. "Were we surprised," Jo added.

The fish turned out to be a large, lake trout, which they poached in their portable oven. From their boat they brought salad fixings and baked potatoes. I furnished a bottle of Seafarer's rum. It turned out to be a beautiful evening, just the three of us on the island, ending with my invitation to come aboard my boat for a latte.

"Every boat should have an espresso maker," I explained. They looked again at my boat — and appeared dubious.

Jo managed to fit into the quarter berth alongside the hatchway, after I shoved some of my stuff under the seat. I perched in front of gear in the forepeak. Lynn sat in the cockpit, looking in.

I steamed the coffee in my cup-sized espresso maker and worked the latte cups.[3] The coffee was much appreciated, but after a short while, Jo got up and excused herself. "I get claustrophobic," she said.

When they left, the night closed on my island paradise. Outside the cove, high winds had come up from somewhere, and on the lake the waves raged.

In here, it was calm and comfortable. The island was beginning to feel like home.

*   *   *

The next day dawned with small craft warnings broadcast on the VHF. It would be sunny, but winds would be moderate to strong westerlies, gusting 40 to 60 kilometers per hour.

That didn't seem like really good sailing weather for my little boat, but the hefty *Timothy Lee* was bound for Silver Islet.

In the cove, gentle waves lapped the wooden piers; the breeze was a gentle caress. I helped the Bradfords shove off and climbed a rocky pinnacle. From my vantage point, the big lake looked blue and beautiful — a Technicolor lake of glacier water, with clouds reflecting in it. But whitecaps on the water told me there was wind.

Minutes later, the *Timothy Lee* headed out from the cove on an easterly course and raised a deeply reefed headsail and then the mainsail. I saw a gust of wind heel the 12-ton sailboat a bit. Their ocean-going cutter was handling the waves fine, but it was a bouncy ride, with the mast cutting a rapid arc back and forth.[4]

I slowly trudged back to the waterfront, feeling a little lonesome.

I was now alone on this remote island.

Time to get a little work done. I pulled out my *Boat Log & Record* and my notebook, and sat opposite my boat on the cantilevered deck. Here, in the shadow of a rock, I had a small, wooden table and a chair I found on the island. I had only begun to record my 4th of July experiences when my pen stopped moving and my mind wandered back to the storm.

I had been lucky to survive.

What a difference an hour would have made! Had my reluctant engine fired right up, I could have departed Grand Portage on schedule.

By the time the storm hit, I'd have been safe in this harbor.

Remembering, I put down my pen. When that wall of wind hit me, it literally picked up my sailboat and shoved it over so far that I thought we were going over all the way. I saw the mast rush down to the water; I saw green water cover the portlight. We teetered there for an eternity; the boat was in the grip of the storm and not coming back up.

My God! How much wind came at me?

What if the boat had gone over all the way? I'd have been in icy water, upside down. I'd have had to swim out and clamber atop that wave-overridden hull. My radio would have been underwater, so I couldn't have called for help. By now I would be drifting out toward the middle of Superior, sitting atop my small boat, shivering and hypothermic.

Maybe not. A thought crossed my mind. I dismissed it.

But moments later, I was back at enumerating what could

have gone wrong. What if that slam-dunk had busted my boat's plastic windows, letting Superior rush in? We'd have been in deep trouble for sure. What if a bigger wallop of water had shot up and over the centerboard trunk, flooding us? What if I did not have my safety harness on and I got swept over the side?

I put down my pen and began to perspire, but not from the heat of the day.

I had been lucky. Nothing broke on the boat. Everything held together. My boat and I had survived.

But we'd only done one day of cruising so far.

We still had the rest of the journey ahead of us.

Photo / Clive Dudley

Snug in Thompson Cove, (left to right) *Chris 'N' Me, Lucky Lady, Rejoyce* and *Persistence* are tied up along the dock. Photo was taken from hill overlooking the cove. Lake Superior is in the background.

Chapter Twelve

RIDERS OF THE
GREEN STORM

They can because they think they can.
— Virgil

FROM THE COVE'S ENTRYWAY came the sound of powerful marine engines. I glanced up from my improvised writing table to see two powerboats, the *Lucky Lady* and *Chris "N" Me*, come charging up to the dock. To the accompaniment of raucous cheering and shouting, engines were shifted into reverse, motors revved, and several burly looking men jumped down to tie the boats to the dock.

Visiting firemen! I grumped. I studied them carefully, not at all willing to lose the tranquility of my island. They were muscular and fit in appearance, and obviously in high spirits. Following them was a hefty-looking sailboat, the *Rejoyce,* out of Thunder Bay.

I gave up trying to jot something down, closed my writing book, and strolled over to see if anyone needed help. They didn't, of course, but it gave me a chance to meet and greet these new visitors to my island. I was thinking of the island in these terms.

They offered me a beer, and as we got acquainted, I found out my visitors actually included some firemen for the city of Thunder Bay, out on holiday.[1]

I stood straighter as I realized that they had just come from where the storm had struck. Just before I encountered high winds, I remembered hearing several maydays broadcast on my boat's radio.

Obviously, something big had ripped through Thunder Bay. A sailboat had been capsized. People tossed into the water.

Maybe they had news.

As we drank beer at dockside, we began to talk. I was surprised to learn these men were in the midst of the Green Storm, as it came to be known.

In fact, one of the boaters had been part of a daring rescue of another boater in distress.

*   *   *

It had all begun very simply.

The Fourth of July had dawned as just another beautiful Sunday at the Thunder Bay Fire Department, the kind this northern Lake Superior city often enjoys, with bright sun and blue skies.

It came a surprise for the firemen to hear a warning from dispatch:

"Something big is coming through."

Hurriedly, they pulled their trucks into the protection of the fire station, and 10 minutes later, they saw a blackness rolling over the western horizon.

When it hit, the sky turned green.

"I never saw the sky like that, absolutely green," Firefighter

Doug Irwin, captain of *Chris "N" Me*, told me. We were aboard his powerboat, and I listened intently.

"The wind and the rain started to come in and it was blowing so hard I thought it was shooting through closed doors," Doug said. "Our hose tower[2] is six stories high, and we had water blowing right through the top door."

He added, "Water poured down steps like someone was up there with a fire hose"

The rain flooded the tower, and they lost power five minutes after 3 p.m. (Thunder Bay time, an hour ahead of Central Standard Time, in the U.S.)

In the midst of the chaos, dispatch reported a boat had capsized outside the breakwaters.

Danger!

The boat was upside down, and there were people in the water.

*   *   *

On north side pier 3, close to the breakwater, Clive Dudley and his wife, Bev, were at their boat, the *Lucky Lady*.

It was a sunny Sunday afternoon, and they were taking the boat's covers off when the sky turned green.

I was now aboard the *Lucky Lady*, bobbing easily in Thompson Cove, and Clive was telling me that he remembered looking up at the sky and commenting, "Wow, look at this," and trying to get the covers back on when the wind and rains hit.

As he and Bev desperately clutched the covers, they saw a sailboat coming toward them, trying to get off Thunder Bay. It was a 20-foot sloop, sails down and the engine roaring, trying to make the entrance of pier. [2]

"All of a sudden, the winds hit the sailboat head on and drove it backwards," Clive said.

"After about 30 feet, we lost visibility because of the rain. We were just hanging on to our cover on the bridge, and about 10 minutes later, the storm eased off slightly, and we climbed into our cabin. As we got in, our dock mate, Bill, yelled that there was a boat capsized in the harbor.

Photo / Brian Matson

At rest along the pier: the plucky *Lucky Lady* skippered by Clive Dudley

"I called him over and started the boat. Bill grabbed the bow line, untied it, and jumped on board.

"Another boater, Jacques, ran over and grabbed the stern line and also jumped on board.

"Bev was already on the radio in the cabin to the Coast Guard about the emergency, asking for assistance, and letting them know we were on our way out there.

"It was still pretty windy, and we had quite a chop. Our boat is very stable, built as an ocean cruiser, but with the winds that day, the boat went over maybe 40 degrees."

Clive paused for a moment in his narration. "But it was just one of those things," he said. "No time to think about it ... you do it.

"We saw three heads in the water, but when we got closer, we saw it was two people and a dog ... no life jackets.

"We made a sweep up to the boat on the leeward[3] side, then came up. Bill and Jacques were able to grab hold of the young couple and their dog and pull them on board.

"They'd been in the water a good 15 minutes, and, of course, looked cold and terrified. We got them into the cabin, where Bev was able to get them dry clothes and blankets to warm them up.

"We made another turn and got a line on the bow of the sailboat, because you don't want to leave a boat out in the middle of the harbor drifting upside down. I tied on the starboard side and started pulling it in, but with the winds and the waves, it was pulling me right into pier, going sideways.

"I gave the engine three quarters throttle, and I was able to get the steering back again, and when I gave it the extra thrust, the sailboat just righted itself. The rigging and mast were damaged, but it swung around, full of water, and so we got back to the marina and secured the boat.

"The people seemed OK, and we wanted them to go to the hospital, but they had experienced enough for one day. They just wanted to go home."

* * *

In the *Lucky Lady's* canvas-covered bridge, I tried to imagine going out in the storm in this small, single-engine power cruiser to rescue the overturned boaters.

"We were the closest boat there," Clive explained. "Any of the boaters down here would have reacted in the same way when they saw what was happening. As soon as there was a need for a boat to go out there, anybody would have done the same thing. Boaters are like that."

I agreed with him, but I did not overlook his modest explanation of his own rescue work.

He also told me later that he learned the woman swept overboard was 13 weeks pregnant. She and the other boaters were in water 10 to 15 minutes — "and that's not warm water. It's Lake Superior we're talking about."

I smiled. I knew.

But everyone realized that had Clive and Bev not gone out there when they did, the ending might have been a lot different.

"As far as I'm concerned, that guy's a real hero," one boater told me later.

I agreed.

* * *

Everyone in the harbor talked about the Green Storm, as it came to be known, and I began to fill in more of the details of what had happened. I realized I would not know them all until I returned from the voyage and I could check various reports.

But everyone who had been through it regarded the storm a real horror story.

It had begun up north of us, somewhere. When the storm roared into Thunder Bay, it had arrived with practically no warning and the sky had turned dark, then green. The rain and winds were fearsome.

Then it surged outward onto the open waters of Superior.

I knew all about that.

I looked at my little, homemade boat, with her tall mast, and remembered with a shudder how we had fought for our very survival in the teeth of the storm. No wonder my boat was blown around so badly. It was possible we had been through the Superior equivalent of "the Perfect Storm."

Worse, from all I'd heard, the storm foreshadowed unsettled, heavy weather ahead.

Superior was preparing quite a voyage for me and my old boat.

I wondered what else I would encounter when I shoved off for Thunder Cape — sailing in the wake of the Green Storm.

Thompson Island has the furthest west of the mysterious Pukaskwa Pits.
Here, Reg Essa checks out one of the rocky depressions.

Chapter Thirteen

MYSTERY OF THE PITS

Knowledge comes,
But wisdom lingers.
—Alfred, Lord Tennyson

TOWARD EVENING, the wind died and the cove's water was smooth as glass, mirroring the pines and the rocky ledges. Boats cast blue shadows in the lowering rays of the sun.

The island was a sort of South Seas paradise — but also an eye-opener for me. I had thought I'd be in a wilderness. Instead, I found a well-developed bit of civilization wrapped up in a tiny, wild enclave, most remarkably, in the mouth of Thunder Cape.

It did not come about by accident. Thunder Bay boaters credited this island's remarkable development to a sailor by the name of Al Wray.

"Al Wray was a real character who liked to party," Doug Irwin, on board *Chris "N" Me*, told me. I learned that Wray was a World War II sailor and battle survivor, who, after cruising the wild shoreline of Thunder Bay, came to Thompson Island. "He liked it because it had a deep bay but was all natural," Doug explained.

Al, his wife, Georgiana, and his friends brought out old lumber lashed to their boats, plank by plank, and began to build the docks. They also used driftwood. When Wray died in 1985, the boaters formed a little group called Friends of Thompson Island and continued building on the island.

"They just go as they get the material," Doug said, sweeping his arm toward the dock. "They stand on the dock and say, 'We can go a little more this way or that.' The dock is about 200 feet long, cantilevered out so that it does not destroy land. They brought out drills and rods to anchor it to the rocks, so that it's environmentally friendly."

"Does the area belong to the boaters?" I asked.

"It's Crown land. It belongs to the Ontario government, and subject to its rules and regulations," Doug explained. "One is that there can be no permanent structure, but the docks are not considered a permanent structure. Neither is the sauna. And all buildings need to be unlocked and accessible to everyone."

Albert Wray is not forgotten. There's a memorial to the sailor high on the north hill overlooking the harbor.

"It's a bit of a climb, but there are ropes to assist, and there's a bench, so you can sit down and look over the harbor," Doug explained. "Al would have loved it."

Doug recalled that Wray used to tell his friends, "When I kick the bucket I'm coming back as a seagull."

When Al died, his family and friends took a boat ride to place his ashes at his favorite place — the hill above us, overlooking the bay. His ashes are buried under a memorial stone beside the bench.

During the 18-mile trip from Thunder Bay, a lone seagull accompanied the boat all the way to Thompson Cove.

"I suspect Al is still spending his time in paradise," Doug said.

* * *

In the lowering rays of the sun, I gazed out of *Rejoyce's* ample portlights. The island stood in dark relief, with the sun throwing shadows. There was a mystery to this island that I wanted to explore.

The so-called Pukaskwa Pits found along the Canadian north shore have been the center of archeological controversy for years. They are ancient, but no one knows exactly how they came about or why.[1] Their use has been lost in the mists of time, but the speculation is that the pits were sites for solitary spirit quests — religious experiences.[2]

"There are pits on the island," I began tentatively.

"Not far," Reg Essa, the boat's skipper, said. "Near the tip of the island."

"What do the pits look like?"

"We'll go over and show you," Reg said. A little later, we were in Doug Irwin's small inflatable, gliding easily over the cove's sheltered waters and past the entryway into Thompson cove. On a point on its northern shore, we ran the inflatable up on the beach. Reg and I scrambled ashore.

We worked our way up a slight incline, past trees and brush, and emerged into a primeval stillness. Ahead of us lay a large clearing composed of smooth stones, some as large as a flattened football, gray in color, and covered partially by lichen. The peculiar roundness of the stones I was standing on suggested they had been smoothed by eons of Superior's wind, rain and waves, and were an ancient part of the lake.

"There they are," Reg said, moving toward a shallow depression. I watched as he picked his way down into a sort of pit until he stood at about waist level. It was about three feet deep, dish-shaped, and about nine feet in length.

I walked around the oval-shaped pit, found a rough stairway on the northern side, and walked down to stand beside Reg. At the bottom were more rocks and gravel.

From my historical information, I knew these pits are the farthest west of these mysterious depressions. But for what were they used?

"One theory is that they were used for shelter," Reg explained. "Whoever dug them would bring their canoes ashore and pull them over the pits."

I crouched down, getting a view of the rim from eye level. In the pit, there was room for several people, perhaps even enough for the crew of a birch-bark canoe.

"By getting down in a pit," Reg said, "a man can get out of wind and get some protection from the elements. These pits occur all along the North Shore."

I tried to imagine pulling an overturned canoe over the pit. A tarp or oilcloth draped on the bottom would complete an emergency shelter.

If I were wind-bound, or caught in a rainstorm, a pit like this would give me a nice, little shelter. It would not exactly be the Hilton, but the stones around me would take the brunt of the weather, and my canoe would be my roof. I'd be out of the wind and rain and probably resting comfortably on packs or furs.

It all made sense. So the pits were shelter pits.[3]

In the golden rays of the setting sun, we left the tip of Thompson Cove. I felt the warmth on my face, but also an inner glow.

Somehow, the ancient structures gave me a connection with those who had preceded me on the Big Lake.

Part Three

INTO THE ISLANDS

Where lies the land
To which the ship would go?
Far, far ahead,
Is all her seamen know.
— Arthur Hugh Clough

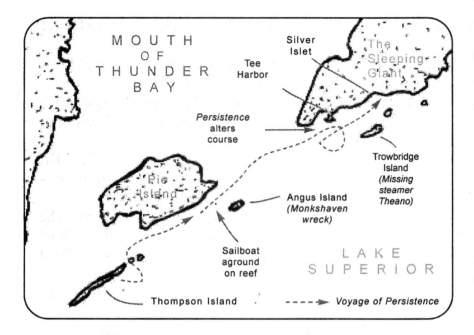

Chapter Fourteen

TO THE ISLAND OF SILVER

You never know what is enough unless
You know what is more than enough.
—William Blake

P ERSISTENCE, PERSISTENCE," the woman's voice came urgently over my VHF. I had the radio volume turned up high to be able to hear it over the sound of wind and waves as we crossed Thunder Cape.

"We have hit a reef and are aground."

I leaned forward, keying my mike. "This is *Persistence*."

I was now in the shadow of the Sleeping Giant, opposite Tee Harbor.[1] It had been a rough crossing, and I was glad to be nearing Silver Islet.

"Can you assist?" she asked. "We're aground in three feet of water."

Her sailboat was on a reef near Angus Island — a reef I had sailed by and had taken great pains to avoid.

"I'm on my way," I said, throwing over the helm and heading back to the rough water.[2] I'd be there in about 45 minutes, I guessed.

But other boaters were monitoring the distress call. "I'll call *Lucky Lady*," Reg aboard *Rejoyce* offered. "A powerboat'll help."

I got on the air again and told Reg I was on my way. The choppy waves of the crossing began to shove my little sailboat around. I wasn't sure what I could do to pull a heavy keelboat off a reef, but I knew I had to try.

"Abort," he said. "You're too far away. There are powerboats in the area."

He was telling me that *Lucky Lady*, the boat that had rescued the overturned sailboat on July 4th, was better for the job. Clive Dudley, its skipper, knew these waters and knew what he was doing.

"I understand," I replied, "And I am resuming my heading."

*   *   *

I was tied up at the dock in Silver Islet when the sailboat arrived with a slightly shaken crew aboard.

"I'm still getting over going aground," the skipper said. "Twenty-five years of boating, and nothing like this has happened before."

"I heard your call. How'd you get off? The power boats?"

"No," he shook his head. "We tried rocking the boat back and forth. Then we tried the boat hook. I saw a little blue water, gave her some gas, and we were off."

"Twenty five years," he repeated. "Nothing like this ever happened before."[3]

*   *   *

The dock at Silver Islet was old and rough. One sailor had warned me about it; moreover, he told me that the most miserable night he'd spent at a dock was at Silver Islet. "It's wide open to the storms from the east," he said, ominously.

I had a position about halfway down the east side of the dock, and after I had put down my fenders, I looked closely at the ancient timbers. They were scoured and worn from decades of ice and water; I saw metal spikes sticking out.

Not the best thing for my little cedar boat. A wave, a slip of the fender, and I'd be impaled.

In search of a "camel." I walked down the dock toward land and saw a pile of lumber behind the old General Store. Sorting through the pile, I found a hefty plank of old wood four inches thick, a foot deep, and ten feet long. I grunted as I lifted it and carried it back to the dock.

Tying a line around either end, I lowered the plank down the pilings to the level of my wooden rub rail. The camel was now in place — a horizontal cross-piece lying across the pilings. From the top of the dock, I lowered as many fenders as I could find aboard my boat. Provided that the camel didn't slip between the pilings, or the fenders didn't get pushed aside, my boat would be secure.

Though the warning about storms from the east remained in my mind, I wasn't too worried. The day was golden sunshine and beautiful waters.

I'd enjoy my time here at Silver Islet.

*   *   *

At sunset, a chill wind blew through the old, mining town. I tuned the VHF to the all-important Canadian weather channel.

"Small craft warning," it reported. "Winds in the east, increasing to 40 knots, becoming southeasterly."

Forty knots of wind would kick up sizeable waves, maybe up to six feet. But I was inside the break wall at the government dock.

I snapped off the radio and glanced to the east. There was a sturdy break wall, but I saw the entryway was wide open to anything that kicked up on the big lake from the east or southeast.

On impulse, I picked up a hand compass to determine the

direction of the wind. The lubber line swung unerringly to the southeast. I'd catch anything that rolled in through that entry-way.

As a trace of wind started to moan in the rigging, I knew I was in for a rough night.

*   *   *

It built slowly, a low moan, then a howl. The boat began rocking back and forth, beam to the wind.

The waves began to roll in.

Night fell like a knife slicing away the light. The harbor and the water became black with the storm. I heard the awful howl of the wind, the clank of gear inside the boat, and increasing-ly, the slam of my hull against the fenders. They groaned against the weight.

Moan, shudder, thump. The boat bucked up against the wood. I sat below, balancing myself, alone in the darkness.

My little boat was getting lifted and slammed into the fend-ers, twisting back and forth. We were in a deadly dance with the wind and waves, the mast swinging one way, then another, fenders groaning. The hull was moving up and down. I was getting dizzy.

Clank! Slam! Groan. My little boat was catching every gust, lifting to every wave peak, dropping to every trough. The motion increased as the storm built. Icy fingers clawed at my boat.

I was fully dressed in long johns and polar fleece, ready to leap out if an emergency flared up. I propped my back against the windward side of the cabin, hoping my weight would ease the pounding. I was growing cold, so I pulled up my sleeping bag.

To help keep out the dreadful cacophony of the storm, I jammed my watch cap down over my ears. It didn't help much.

In the constant motion, my ankle hurt. I braced it on a pile of clothing, but a dip and a slam up against the piers, and the ankle would move. Pain would shoot up. The no-aspirin aspirin only succeeded in diminishing the ache.

From time to time, I moved over to the portlight facing the

dock to shine a light out. I could see the hull working up and down and sideways, against the fenders.

Would the camel hold? What if the boat tipped too much, catching her beam under the board. What if...

Fears coursed through my mind at every new sound or creak, every big buck and lunge of the hull under me.

It was a bad night.

At about 1:30 a.m., I awoke, startled. I had slept fitfully, my mind entertaining ghosts of frightening thoughts.

"We're going under," one ghost had shouted. My body tensed. We had been swept under the pier and lay helplessly upside down in the water.

It had been a dream, but I was shaken. My heart pounding, I threw off the sleeping bag and grabbed for my flashlight.

I stopped. My fears were getting to me. I'd checked the fenders, the camel, the lines – everything — time and time again.

I had done everything I could. But I could not move the boat in this storm. I could not leave the boat and sit up on that dock.

I'd just have to ride it out.

I fell asleep, shivering in the chill.

*   *   *

At first light, I wakened fitfully and I looked out at the harbor. It was gray out there, but I could see dark waters tipped with whitecaps rolling in.

Daylight brought new faith to me — in my boat and myself.

We had survived another one. I said a silent prayer.

From the old mining town, the legendary island of silver can be seen through the trees. Though the island is abandoned, some say the silver is still down there.

Chapter Fifteen

RICH LIFES OF SILVER ISLET

The machine does not isolate man from the great problems of nature, but plunges him more deeply into them.
— Antoine DeSaint-Exupery

MORNING. I checked my face in the small mirror and winced. A haggard, white reflection looked back. I could see shadows under my eyes from lack of sleep and a pinched expression on my face. My hair was pasted down from my watch cap. I was still shivering in my long underwear, polar fleece, and heavy boot socks.

"But the long night is over," I reminded myself as I threw open my hatch. That damned storm!

A patter of rain greeted me. It was a dark, wet day — more

joy. I groggily clambered aboard the dock and slowly straight-
ened myself up, painfully working the kinks out of my body.
I'd felt crappy before, but now it seemed as if my entire body
was hurt.

A dock worker saw me. "Another gray day," he observed,
not unkindly. "Might as well get used to it up here."

"I'm adjusting," I said, ambling off the wet dock and onto
the wetter land. To the north loomed the giant mountain of legend, and at water's edge, the sleepy little hamlet of Silver
Islet.[1]

Just to be out and stretching my legs seemed to be helping.
I began to feel better as I hobbled uphill to the main street.
These days, downtown Silver Islet features an old, wooden
General Store, and a narrow street at the base of a high cliff.
At water's edge were some old cabins. Not a lot of room, but
scenic.

I was in search of an old friend. It did not take a long walk
before I knocked on a cabin door. Jim Coslett, a large, white-
haired man, greeted me. Jim is the resident expert on the island
that lies just beyond sight — the one that had catapulted this
tiny town into international fame.

In fact, I learned that he and a friend had taken their sailboat, *The Barb*, out to circle the island the day I had arrived at
the dock. Going to the island was like a homecoming for Jim,
for he had been brought out to Silver Islet as a boy and had
spent nearly every summer in this hamlet. Jim knew first-hand
the tales of the old miners.

Jim and I left his cottage and headed eastward on the hamlet's single road along the shore. A small island came into
view, beyond Burnt Island. Even from a mile away I could
make out the flat surface with scrub-like trees blossoming on
it.

This is the abandoned island of silver, once the richest and
most unusual silver mine in the world.

It's pretty much the way they found it back in 1867, Jim told
me. The trees have grown a great deal, hiding what was once
bare rock.

But the mine is still down there. And so is the silver.

*   *   *

It was probably from where I stood that several men rowed out in July 1868 to the unimpressive hunk of rock 90 feet across, 8 feet at its highest, and polished smooth by Superior's storms. It was simply designated as Island No.4.

The survey party was on a thankless task. This godforsaken North Shore wilderness was owned by the Montreal Mining Company, but the Canadian government was going to levy a two-cents-an-acre tax. The men's job was to figure out which of the several thousands acres around Thunder Cape[1] were worth keeping.

Headed by Thomas Macfarlane, the four men had been out since mid-May, checking on mining opportunities throughout the Thunder Bay area. They had spent thankless weeks looking for "copper-silver ores" on Jarvis Island. They had followed the shoreline in their Mackinaw boat, visiting other islands and blasting out samples of ore.

But on the western side of this island, one of the men saw something shiny in the water. It was a startling white line contrasting with the dark ore — 20 feet at its widest, running from the rock into the lake.

Excitedly, they scrambled into the cold water and pried out pure silver.

It was an incredible find, but a real problem. There was all that silver, but it was below Lake Superior.[2] Access to its veins could be reached only through this small island about the size of a house.

Miners soon found storms rolling out of the southeast would overrun the island, tear away protective cribs, and even slash away solid rock. After repeated failures to get at the silver, the mining company sold the mine for $225,000 to American industrialist Alexander Sibley.

Sibley hired the boldest mining engineer he could find, Captain William Belle Frue, who arrived by boat in 1870. Frue built a rock pile six feet high on the islet and climbed to the top to study the lake's action.

When a violent storm rose from the unprotected southeast, he watched the waves build and march toward his tiny rock pile. He was stranded.

It was only after the storm had blown itself out that a row-boat could come from shore to rescue the freezing engineer.

Duly impressed, Frue got to work and built a virtual fortress around the island. Twenty-thousand square feet of heavy timbers became a six-foot-high break wall, held by iron shafts two inches thick.

Another storm slammed into the fortress; waves overran the break wall. That night from the mainland, Frue peered into the darkness at his besieged fortress.

When the storm waters subsided, Frue rowed out to see that Superior had demolished 200 feet of breakwater, torn open a coffer dam, and filled the mine shaft. The two-inch-thick iron rods were so bent that a miner half-joked: "They might as well have been my wife's hairpins."

Frue rebuilt the tiny island again, this time encircling it with a crib of timber filled with rock to break the waves. Men worked 18-hour days to make it rise 18 feet above the lake, with a base that extended 75 feet.

He expanded the island to ten times the size of the original rock. On the cribwork and island were the shaft house, four large boardinghouses, machine shops, blacksmith and carpenter shops, a boiler room, offices and clubrooms, a lighthouse, a system of range lights, storehouses, and sturdy buildings filled with mining machinery, huge engines, and massive docks. The mine employed 480 men.

Silver Islet boomed. Between 1872 and 1874, nearly a million ounces of silver ore was taken out. The stock of the company rose from $50 a share to $25,000. Speculators made a fortune on the stock.

But as the mine went deeper, the shaft cut through fissures and water began to pour in. Miners shored up the cracks as best they could and brought in heavier water pumps. The battle against Superior had begun in earnest.

Storms slammed out of the southeast. One December gale

battered the fortress and carried away 350 feet of cribbing, 20,000 feet of lumber, and tons of huge boulders. Superior picked up huge rocks and tossed them about like hailstones.

Miners worked cold and wet, living with the constant danger of flooding. They descended in a cage deep below Superior's surface, the flickering illumination of their head candles reflecting on the dripping walls.

Would a dammed-up fissure give way? Would waves crash through the break walls and drown the shaft and the miners?[3]

For their hardships, the miners were paid $68 a month and were docked $14 for room and board. Each time they left the island they were searched bodily.[4]

The area boomed. In only two years, the shoreline boasted a church (complete with widow's walk around its steeple), schoolhouse, store, post office, and housing for five hundred men. The General Store was built.

The silver community became known for its lavish hospitality and its society. The officers and directors of the company had their own yacht, the *Silver Spray*. The fantastic mining find was widely acclaimed in Europe; once again, bold men had wrestled a fortune out of the harsh North Country.

Below the surface, the mine[5] reached a depth of 1,230 feet. Fifteen levels intersected the main shaft. The lode became elusive, sometimes narrowing, then widening. Huge pumps ran continuously.

In 1884, the mine came to an end. One story, favored by local historians, is that the islet's supply of coal for the pumps lay on board a steamer, immobilized at Houghton, Michigan. Its drunken captain had allowed the vessel to become frozen in.

On the islet, desperate miners fed their boilers every piece of wood they could bring over from the mainland, but by March, the lake was gaining. In the end, the fires went out and the pumps stopped. Lake Superior claimed its own.

Another, less romantic version of the tale is that the mine became unprofitable. The miners were forced to go deeper and farther for less ore, at greater expense and danger.

In 1884, when the price of silver dropped, the mine became too expensive to operate.[6]

The world's richest underwater silver mine was dead.

* * *

"They were getting into very expensive mining at 1,200 feet down," Jim told me. "It was difficult to dewater it. At times they had flooding, and they couldn't control it. They tried wood timbering, but under the pressure, it didn't hold."

He shook his head. "If the mine were a little more productive, perhaps something could have been done. But the veins were pinching out."

"Is some silver still down there?" I asked.

Jim nodded. He told me over the years scuba divers looked over opportunities to take silver out of the mine from columns and walls.

I remembered a conversation I had with his sister, Ann Drynan.

"Nobody knows how much silver is still there," she told me. "They say that when the original miners got down so far, they carved pillars and roofs out of almost solid silver. But these days, since it's underwater, if you take the roof or a pillar out, you are doomed."

Ann continued, "I talked with some skin divers — they're not allowed down there, you know — but they were there anyway, taking pictures. They saw picks and shovels just sticking out of the walls where the miners had left them, but they couldn't touch anything for fear of bringing it all down on them."

I also had met several divers who had penetrated the shaft. "You go down the main shaft and into one of the side tunnels," one of them told me, "and what you come across are a lot of timbers blocking your way."

A look of concern came over his face.

"I got part way through several timbers, but then stopped. They felt a little loose to me. You realize that if you dislodge one, the whole works can come crashing down on your head."

He added, "Underwater, that kind of makes you think."

It had made him thoughtful enough to leave. I didn't blame him.

These days, it's hard to believe this hunk of rock was once the world's greatest silver mine. It's a privately held island, and visitors are officially discouraged from stepping foot there, much less visiting the open mine.

Though the silver is still down there, the mine has no iron grates or steel bars blocking the entryway itself.

There's only an open hole. But I am told that if you look down, you can see the clear, cold waters of Superior guarding their own.

*   *   *

It was 6 p.m., my agreed-upon time to rendezvous with home. I looked forward to my call.

Tonight would be a special treat. I'd be using a real telephone with a secure connection and not just my boat's radio. I had located a pay telephone in the back hallway of the General Store.

I began punching in numbers — and suddenly stopped.

It was the most stupid thing, but I could not remember my own telephone number.

I pulled out my wallet, but I didn't have my business cards, or, for that matter, my home telephone number written anywhere.

Dumbfounded, I hung up the receiver and stood in the hallway for a few moments, trying to remember, but with no results. What was wrong, anyway?

Time ticked away. Suddenly, I took out my ballpoint pen and tried printing the number. That was working. Slowly, between pauses, my home telephone number came back to me.

I took no chances. I placed the scrap of paper in front of me and carefully punched in the numbers.

"Glad to hear from you," came the welcome voice of my wife. "How are you?"

"Fine," I said. "Just fine." I decided not to worry her about my strange lapse of memory. I also did not want her to hear about the terrible night I just spent at the dock.

"Up here there's a little rain, but it'll go away in a day or two."

"Did you get any sleep?"

"A little," I said. "Mostly toward dawn," I added carefully. "But the boat is fine. And so am I, *now*."

It may have been stretching a point, but I was truthful.

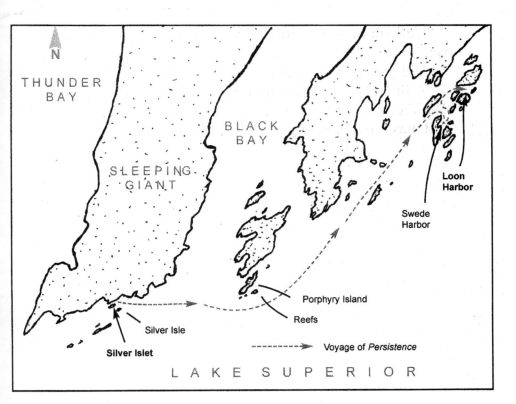

Chapter Sixteen

LURE OF
LOON HARBOR

*Boats are safe in harbor, but that's not
what boats are made for.*
—Boat Log & Record

I AWAKENED WITH A SENSE OF DREAD. Something was wrong; I sat bolt upright and glanced out the portlight.

The sun was shining — a gorgeous day, the kind I'd been waiting for. I unzipped my dodger and stuck my head out. A light breeze riffled through my uncombed hair. In the distance, the water looked blue and inviting.

I was alone on the dock. The other boats were gone.

I checked my watch: 9:30 a.m. I had overslept.

Hastily, I got the boat ready and then swung the 5-horse-power Nissan into the water. I gave a quick pull to the starter chord and the little beauty fired right up. A good omen.

The sun shone brightly as I motored past the break wall. Although I was late starting out, I enjoyed a fine sense of adventure. My spirits were high.

Today I'd be entering the island archipelago of the proposed world's largest marine freshwater conservation area. I would need to be cautious. Every few years, people and boats enter this wilderness area and disappear.

I'd gone over my route with Jim, who suggested several possible islands to spend the night. Coming up was Swede Island, with a small dock.

"Loon harbor," he had told me in his understated way, "was worth a visit." He'd been there many times.

I had my GPS coordinates punched in for my route. I'd head out of Silver Islet, here on the tip of the Sibley Peninsula, and slip through a small channel between the peninsula and Skinaway Island. I had a waypoint to steer me south of Porphyry Reef, lying to the south of Porphyry Island. Nasty looking business — I'd give it plenty of sea room. From there, I'd head northeasterly past Dreadnought Island.

I decided to sail inside the Shaganash Island cut, despite the abundance of reefs. My next waypoint would be the channel between Swede and Gourdeneau islands, taking care to sail north of some reefs opposite Macoun Island.

To the north, between Spain Island and Basher Island was Loon Harbor — and a lot of rocks.

I had punched in my GPS for Loon at a 48.31.6N, 88.30 9W entry. I was taking no chances of repeating my error of not finding the entryway as I had done at Thompson Cove. I also marked the coordinates on the chart.

I congratulated myself. I was getting smarter.

*   *   *

One hand on the tiller, I cruised past Burnt Island and Cross

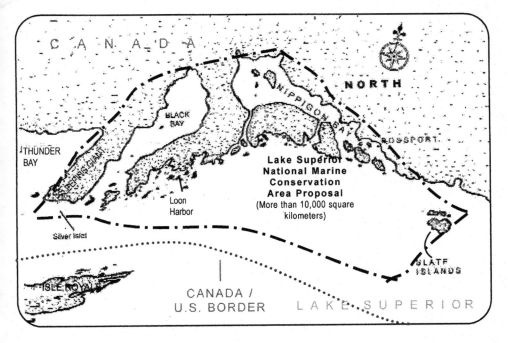

Rock, and as I made my way around Sibley Cove, I had a last, good look at the old silver mine.

From my cockpit, I could see the low-lying rock was open to the full sweep of storms. I could not help but marvel at the determination and persistence of the old-time miners on "skull rock" so far out on Superior.

As I made my turn around Sand Island, the wind had picked up, with the seas fetching from the southeast. We began our dance with the wind and waves.

No question about it. We were on the open waters of Superior.

My boat was handling the seas just fine, though I was a little tense in the teeter-totter ride. We'd slice through a trough, then a wave would come up and hit us on the starboard with a little shove, and we'd slowly go up and down, as well as a little sideways.

I'd brace myself in the cockpit, tensing my body to counteract the motion, hand on the tiller feeding a little bow into the wave, and letting us fall off. Then we'd slide past — and resume our dance.

It seemed to me that the wind was increasing. My cockpit seat was about 18 inches above the waterline, so any waves above one meter would be well above my boat's freeboard.

Today, we'd have waves of one to two meters (about three to six feet high) on the average. Unexpressed, but what every boater knows, is that there would be a lot of un-average waves, when some waves combined. These would create waves up to 50 percent higher.

Crossing the Montreal Channel, we were making about 6 m.p.h., a fine speed in these cross winds. I gave the point on Porphyry Island and Porphyry Reef a wide berth, though it was really difficult to figure out where the reefs exactly were located.

All I knew was they were under me, somewhere, and I really didn't want to find them — this would be a lousy place to run into a rock. I decided to stand at least a half mile offshore.

I was using Canadian Hydrographic Service chart 2301, Passage Island to Thunder Bay, with information printed both in English and French. Canadian charts give depths in fathoms, not feet, and water less than three fathoms are tinted blue. Various tiny numbers dotted the blue areas, and it seemed to me that the detailed Canadian chart had an awful lot of blue where I was going.

The vista around me was changing. I was now getting into one of the Big Lake's most beautiful cruising areas, but this came at the cost of being in one of the most reef-punctuated parts of the lake.

We had changed directions, heading to the northeast. I glanced at my GPS; we had picked up speed, recording 6.1 and even 6.5 m.p.h.

I was getting my navigational heading from my GPS unit, ignoring my compasses, for good reason. To the north of me, past Edward Island, was Magnet Island, and beyond that, Magnet Point. On my chart, stamped in purple ink, was an area of "Magnetic Disturbance/Anomalie magnetique."

That meant my compasses could be wildly off. So I steered by the GPS, the satellites as my guide.

*   *   *

In the distance, coming from off Shaganash Island, was a sail. As it drew closer, I lifted my binoculars. It was a cutter rig, deeply reefed: my friends, the Bradfords in their big cutter, *Timothy Lee*.

A pleasant surprise out here. I hailed them on the radio, and I saw Jo Ann wave. We exchanged brief pleasantries, and then they were heading away from me.

The interlude was past and I felt alone once again.

*   *   *

Waves were now smashing against my beam in small explosions of white. Foam slopped over the cockpit coaming, giving me a shower.

The wind had definitely come up — hard.

The good news was that I was really flying along, getting a little help from the wind and waves. My GPS was now registering 6.9 m.p.h. Outstanding for a little sailboat!

I flew into the channel between Spain and Gourdeau Island, getting some protection from the waves. But the wind had turned this wide channel almost smoky; tips of waves were foaming off.

Though the chart showed the channel to be relatively reef free, we were still doing 5.6 miles per hour — much too fast.

Wind was driving us, even under the patch of sail I was carrying. The only answer I could think of was that the winds were being channeled by the islands. What had been a beam wind now became a following wind.

I moved in closer to Swede, set a course on the automatic helm, and dropped my mainsail.

In these strong following winds, heading for a harbor, sail would be more of a hindrance than a help. I would run under the iron wind — my outboard.

I studied my chart. Swede Island harbor looked land-locked on three sides, which would give me a lot of protection from these winds. I had heard there was a small dock inside this harbor as well as a sauna. Visions of wonderful Thompson Cove swum into mind.

But I had been warned the harbor had shallow water at its entryway and only shallow-draft boats could enter. That didn't seem like a problem. I was certainly shallow draft, especially if I pulled my steel centerboard up.

I moved ahead with the automatic helm on remote control. I could stand up coming into Swede harbor, peering down into the water. My boat would do the work; I'd just guide it.

I turned down the engine to a crawl. Anxiously, I stood atop my cockpit seat, shielding my eyes against the sun.

Was this the harbor?

In the distance, near the water's edge, was a small shack. That had to be the sauna. And, yes, I could see a small dock sticking out into the water. It was deserted.

I began to make my move, pulling the centerboard up part way, reading my depth sounder. I watched it go from 4 to 2 and then down, down to zero. That meant that I had roughly four and a half feet under my actual keel.[1]

I felt that odd, little halting motion and a sort of sibilant hiss. I was bottoming out.

I jumped back and grabbed the tiller. I wanted to feel what I was doing. Even if I had my centerboard up, I'd ground out at about three feet with my rudder.

I circled around, trying again to find the channel. I couldn't see it because of the shadows and the wind.

I eased inward, tensing up. If I went aground in this wilderness area, I'd be in trouble.

That hissing sound came again and I felt the tiller vibrate in my hand. We were grounding out.

I shoved my engine in reverse and gunned it — hoping it was in time.

Slowly, engine growling and water spraying, we backed off.

It was time for plan two, which was to quit screwing around and get the hell out of here.

Under power, I smartly headed back into the channel. It was when I emerged past the northern tip of Swede that I caught the full brunt of the winds once again and the smoky seas. Something was really howling out here. I turned up the wick on the engine once more, and made my turn.

With the wind and seas behind us, we soared past Rex Island up north along Spain Island, and at it tip, between Lasher and Spain, I turned eastward again.

Carefully watching my GPS landmark, I entered a cut guarded by lofty islands, their bases awash with waves and their sides covered with dark-green fir trees.

Loon Harbor. As I ducked in, the hills took the brunt of the blast, and I emerged into a changed world. Here was calm. Peace. Beautiful skies, sparkling, blue water.

As I moved deeper into the small harbor, I cut my engine power to barely turning over and engaged the autopilot with its remote. Standing in the cockpit, I slowly circled the end of the harbor, peering down into the clear depths.

I checked the depth sounder. I had about 10 feet beneath my keel. The water I was floating upon was near enough to be in the shadow of the islands — and relatively calm. I watched breezes riffle and play upon its surface, but there were no waves.

A little bit of heaven! This was one of the best anchorages I'd ever been in.

One by one, I dropped my two Danforths from the bow and watched them sink in the clear water. They settled in at an angle about 20 degrees off each side of my bow.

I eased the engine into reverse and let one anchor line, then the other, play out in my hands. When I had about 75 feet out, I wrapped the lines around cleats.

The boat slowed, then stopped as the anchors dug in and held.

We were home for the night, double anchored and secure. I could relax.

I moved back to the dodger, and out of habit, checked my GPS.

It was blank!

The batteries had gone dead. It had faithfully guided me into harbor, then gave up.

Not its fault. Mine. I should have been more careful.

*   *   *

Cradling my trusty GPS, I closed up the dodger and went below, more than a little tired. I slumped in my forward bunk, feeling the sensation of being at anchor.

This was the first time I had the hook down during this voyage. I felt almost lyrical as I treated myself to a shot of Seafarer's rum and began to enjoy myself.

No longer am I awkwardly tied alongside a pier, jostled by the waves and punched repeatedly against the timbers, the fenders groaning — at war with a storm, trying to survive with our tenuous hold onto the land.

Here, there is the hum of wind in the rigging and the gurgling sounds of water going past my hull. It was hard to believe that outside my little harbor, there is quite a windstorm raging.[2]

After a while, the red sun begins to go down. The red orb becomes my beacon as we glide smoothly back and forth. The islands fall into shadow and become black.

Persistence is in her element, tugging playfully at her anchor.

I also have changed. I am no longer a creature of land — but of the sea.

As darkness comes into my wilderness harbor, I grow drowsy. My last impressions are of being rocked gently, tenderly by the wind in my cradle.

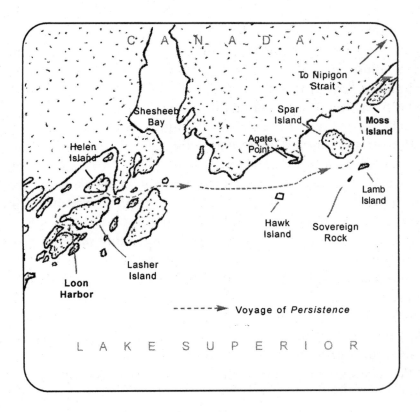

C A N A D A

To Nipigon Strait

Shesheeb Bay

Spar Island

Moss Island

Helen Island

Agate Point

Lamb Island

Hawk Island

Sovereign Rock

Lasher Island

Loon Harbor

- - - - - ▶ Voyage of *Persistence*

L A K E   S U P E R I O R

Chapter Seventeen

VOYAGE TO MOSS ISLAND

*The day shall not be up so soon as I
To try the fair adventure of tomorrow.*
—William Shakespeare

I AWAKENED EARLY IN THE MORNING to the weak sun's feeble
rays and checked my alarm clock. Odd. The clock showed
2:15 a.m. — and then I remembered it had flown across my
cabin during that 4th of July storm and crashed. But my wristwatch told me it was 6:30 a.m.

Better. I had slept well, hanging at anchor. But it was time
to see what the day would bring. Groggily, I peered out the

portlight. The harbor was gray, with a gray sky and low-hanging clouds over the island.

Not too encouraging, but I needed to get moving. Time to get the kinks out of my body and down no-aspirin aspirins to take care of my knee and ankle.

The pain-killers I had taken last night before I went to sleep had worn off. My left ankle was aching, my knees creaked, and my muscles were stiff and sore.

I had slept in my long underwear, wool socks, and pile fleece and in the morning's chill, none of this seemed too warm. In minutes, my little butane stove took the chill off the tiny cabin as I prepared my morning latte. I unwrapped myself from the sleeping bag and began moving about.

I leaned over to turn my VHF to the all-important Canadian weather forecast. I felt a twinge of trepidation, since I never knew what would be happening on my patch of Superior. Apparently, the forecasters also had difficulty.

A blurt of noise, and there was the Canadian weatherman. I listened carefully, pulling out my *Boat Log & Record* to write down the forecast. Today I'd have alternating sunny and cloudy skies, with 30- to 40- kph winds midday out of the west. Wind would diminish to 20 in the evening.

That seemed acceptable. I liked the part about the partly sunny skies.

Monday I'd have showers or storms. Tuesday would be thunderstorms increasing and windy. Wednesday had a chance of storms.

Not so good — but what else was new?

I glanced again at my notes. Today would start sunny, cloudy and windy, but at least no rain.

I sipped my latte gratefully and made a small resolution. I would not listen to weather forecasts before I had my morning coffee.

While I was sipping, I hauled out my GPS and almost patted it like a pet. It took only a few moments to refill the little unit with fresh batteries, good for about another 20 hours. I'd have to calculate battery use a little better.

I would also have to ration my water. This morning, making coffee, I found that my five-gallon water jug had sprung a leak. One corner was bent up and cracked. This must have happened during yesterday's windstorm.

About half the water had leaked somewhere, but when I looked in the bilge, I found it all right. A little work with my boat sponge got rid of the water through the open centerboard slot, where it mingled with the lake.

I decided I'd try out my new foul weather gear. The Thunder Bay sailors wore theirs a lot, even on land, and I was late in trying mine out.

I hauled the heavy bag out from under the bunk, reminding myself I should have been wearing this heavy duty gear when I got caught in the 4th of July storm. But the storm had been upon me so suddenly and so fiercely, I didn't have a chance to change — only to hang on.

The red-and-blue bib-overalls slid heavily over my jeans and my thermals, topping my polar fleece. I pulled my sea boots over my wool socks.

I tugged on the foul weather parka, snapped down the wrist water guards, zipped and velcroed the front, and pulled the hood in place over my long-billed, black baseball cap. I could velcro, snap, and zip that sucker down so tight a North Atlantic gale couldn't wet me down.

Over the heavy parka, I put on my all-important safety harness, and above that, my equally important floatation device.

I grinned. Today I was ready for anything on Superior.

As I made my out of my hatch, I got a surprise. Rain started to fall and then pelt down, hard. But in my superb foul weather gear, it didn't bother me so much as screw up my faith in yet another day's forecast.

I started the Nissan, let it warm up, then sort of waddled forward to the bow and pulled up the Danforths. They came up easily, but with a lot of mud, which got all over the teak deck and my new foul weather gear.

No worries, it was raining, wasn't it? The mud would wash off. And my beautiful, heavily made foul weather gear was keeping me so warm and dry I was beginning to perspire.

I stowed the anchors below and took over the helm. I wanted to keep going during the early morning hours; a little precipitation wouldn't bother the boat, or me. Besides, rain would keep the winds down.

My destination today was Moss Island.

*   *   *

Under power, we moved smartly westward, rounded the tip of Lasher Island, and began heading northeastward. The day brightened as Helen Island came into view, and I began to worry because at the northernmost part of Lasher, I had to thread my way through several small islands and several reefs.

You took a left, then a right, and you watched for a string of rocks that led down under you. I slowed just a bit, watching the numbers on the depth sounder, and pushed on through.

I began making good time. I was back to 6.9 m.p.h. on my GPS as I exited the islands and headed into deep waters, setting a course to Hawk Island.

A weak sun came out and by 10:30 a.m., I was sweltering. As I moved about, I seemed to squish. Sweat ran down my nose. My heavy foul weather gear was not letting my body's perspiration out. I felt like I was inside a sauna.

I didn't want to strip off all my gear while I was underway, but I did take off the heavy foul weather jacket. I immediately put back on my floatation device and clipped into my safety harness. Under the heavy bib pants, held to my chest by suspenders, I still sweltered.

The day turned to sunshine as I swung by Agate Cove and Agate Point, staying well clear of the reefs to their south. I checked my GPS, my plotting on my chart, as well as my time, and I figured I was still a ways from Spar Island. Along this rugged stretch of islands, I was having difficulty determining which island was which.

Ahead, I saw that Lamb Island was preceded by some ugly looking customers called Sovereign Rock. I checked my chart: these were surrounded by a lot of blue. Blue meant reefs.

The waves now were up and moving, blown up by the morning winds. They'd get worse as the day progressed, but I was nearly at my destination.

Turning north past Spar Island, I headed toward the spectacular scenery of the Nipigon Strait. Ahead lay Fluor Island, with a smaller island to my left. This was Moss Island, where I planned to stay the night.

Heavy woods surrounded me as I entered the channel. In my cruising guide, I had read about a dock at which to tie up, envisioning maybe another Thompson Cove. The dock area was opposite a sand beach, and I was warned of a shoaling of the waters.

I stood up in the cockpit, the remote in one hand and the motor on slow speed as I moved up the narrowing channel. My depth sounder started to show a shallowing, then seemed to bottom out as we approached the narrow area. I saw a few poles in the water, marking the edge of the channel, and I heard the sound of my centerboard kissing sand.

I threw the helm over, getting us further over to the western side of the shoal. That seemed to do the trick. We had a foot or two of water under the centerboard and slid through.

Finding the dock and camp was a little more difficult. I slowly moved past a rustic-looking shack, with pilings in the water and, some boards stuck atop them. A dock?

I took over the helm, and nosed closer, one hand on the throttle. Some of the pilings had fallen into the water. It looked like maybe I could make it in there, but I just didn't trust what might lie beneath my wooden bottom.

I looked hard at the broken down dock. What if another storm came up, like the one I had encountered at Silver Bay when waves pounded me up against the dock?

I put the engine in reverse and backed out. I moved up the channel to look for a better overnight stay

The sun was high. I was sweating buckets in my foul weather bib overalls, but there was really nothing I could do. In this channel, I wanted to keep going.

The cruising guide had warned me the passage along the western side of Moss should be made only with a shallow draft boat and with "local knowledge," since there were shallows and underwater rocks strewn about.

I moved ahead until I passed by a small cove in the island. It was a beautiful little spot, maybe half a mile or so from the northernmost tip of the island, off the channel and in a pristine bit of wilderness. I cruised in slowly, standing high in the cockpit, hanging onto the boom.

The water shallowed, but it felt good. It looked good.

I circled the harbor several times, trying to find where I wanted to be for the night, then dragged out my two Danforths. I put the engine in neutral, then glided forward and dropped my anchors in a 45-degree pattern. The little engine roared in reverse, and the anchors dug in — and held.

I settled back in the cockpit, the sun shining high, and stripped off my bottom foul weather gear. My jeans and long underwear were soaked through with perspiration, but I was happy .

It was a splendid little cove, in a splendid little channel, alongside a splendid little island. We were secure and home for the night.[1]

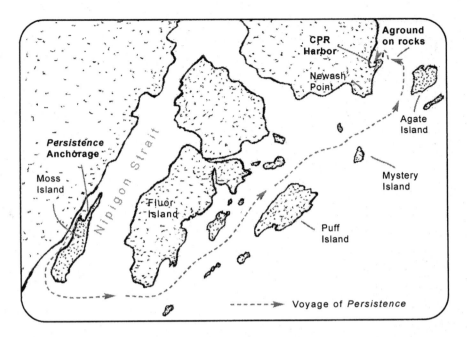

Persistence
Anchorage

Moss
Island

Nipigon Strait

Fluor
Island

CPR
Harbor

Newash
Point

Aground
on rocks

Agate
Island

Mystery
Island

Puff
Island

- - - - ➤ Voyage of *Persistence*

Chapter Eighteen

AGROUND!

*Do what you can, with what
you have, where you are.
—Theodore Roosevelt*

ORNING. I THREW OPEN THE HATCH and blinked happily in the warm sunlight.

In my cove, the water was blue and gentle, a veritable pond of paradise. In its crystalline depths, I could see the sandy bottom beneath my keel. To the south, heavily wooded Moss Island seemed still asleep in the early morning.

But to the north, a heavy cloud hung over the hill overlooking the channel. I studied it for a moment, trying to figure out what it portended.

Rain? Fog? I could not tell.

And, frankly, I did not much care. Bully for me. After all these days of worry and concern, I was in a great mood. I had a great night's sleep at anchor, and I had already decided I would be traveling today, no matter what.

True to my pledge, I stayed away from the radio until I fixed myself a cup of latte and downed a couple of no-aspirin aspirins. Breakfast of champions!

The VHF informed me that a small craft warning was being issued. Blustery winds out of the southwest gusting to 50 kph.

I decided to leave early, before the winds really got going.

Both Danforths came out of the bottom easily, and I shook them up and down in the water to clean them before stowing them away in the bilge. Their weight would once again add to my ballast. The Nissan fired up on the first pull and we began to move south down the channel.

I glanced up. The odd gray plume atop the hill had disappeared. Warmth permeated the water, the beginning of a beautiful day.

But I was not unmindful of Murphy's Law, which postulates that anything that can go wrong will. Murphy's Law for boaters says that anything that can go wrong will — at the worst possible time. And when you least expect it.

But I was having a good time in the islands, and it seemed to me that the worst was behind me. From now on, things would only get better.

As I made my way down the channel, I keyed my mike to the Thunder Bay Coast Guard to file my sail plan with them. I had one hand on the tiller, the other holding my mike.

What was my destination today?

I replied, "CPR Harbor."

"Your ETA?"

I glanced at my chart to estimate my time of arrival.

The radio added, "You know ... what time do you want us to come looking for you?

I laughed. "Thanks," I said.

Still, his explanation had an ominous ring to it. It was on my mind long after I gave him my ETA.

*   *   *

My path lay around Moss Island and across the mouth of the

Nipigon Strait. I'd slip westward past the tip of Fluor Island, avoiding Dacres Rock. I'd go up a sort of channel of islands: past Puff Island and Mystery Island to southwest of Agate Island, where I'd head northward.

Here it would get tricky. My Canadian chart showed a lot of shallowing and there were a bunch of little asterisk-shaped dots. These meant reefs.[1]

Getting into CPR Slip was going to be a little tricky.

*   *   *

I zipped along the inside passage of islands, protected from the lake. High, steep bluffs of pine rose on either side of me. The wind was light so far this morning, but growing. The waters were blue, the sun shone down, and we were having a beautiful time, my little boat and I.

I crossed north of Mystery Island and gave a wide berth to the rocks of St. Ignance Island's Newash Point. Off my port bow lay Agate Island. To the north and west was CPR Harbor, on St. Ignace Island.

I shrugged. Despite the rocks, I'd be OK. I'd just take it easy going in.

As I neared my turn, I found little comfort from my cruising guidebook, which told me about numerous, but unmarked shoals that the author and others had found over the years. The book told me to exercise great care in finding my way into the slip.

I throttled back to about quarter engine speed.

But with the wind behind us, we didn't slow down a lot. We were getting a nice little boost in speed — the wind was coming up.

I turned on the autopilot and with its remote in one fist I stood atop the cockpit seat and braced myself against the boom. From my height, I could see ahead and deep into the water.

There! That had to be the spit of land that led to the harbor. I steered toward it. I knew my passage was supposed to be near the shoals and that I had to hug the shore.

Off my bow, rocks appeared under the water. My depth

sounder rose from one foot under the keel — to zero feet.

Where was the channel that would take me into the harbor?

There was a hollow bump noise, a scraping sound. The tiller twitched in my hand, and I was shoved forward against the boom.

Desperately, I threw the engine into reverse and gave it the gun. No help at all.

I was aground.

The wind piled us against the rocks and, the boat turned sideways, pinioned by the centerboard. Whump! Whump! The wind and the waves began to grind us into the reefs.

I stole a quick glance under the stern. There wasn't enough clearance above the rocks for the prop. I snicked the gear into neutral, turned off the engine, and hoisted it up. I didn't want to also lose an engine.

Grabbing my small Danforth from below, I ran to the bow and threw the anchor out toward deeper water. It did not go far, so I hauled it back and tried again with an underarm swing. Farther.

After it sank, I yanked hard. The anchor popped loose. In the rocks, its flukes would not catch.

I tried several more times, with similar results. Each time the anchor failed to set in the rocks. I could not pull myself off.

Bump! Bam! I did not like the way the boat was caught sideways on the centerboard. Too much wind pressure.[2]

I yanked up on the centerboard pennant, raising the centerboard. Persistence righted herself — and slid further onto the reefs. My friend the wind had helped do that.

Damn! I stood helplessly on deck, sweltering from my exertions, wondering what to do next. The rocky shore was close — maybe 100 feet away.

The wind was increasing as I began pacing the deck, peering down, looking for a way to escape.

Rocks surrounded me. I seemed to be in a pocket of them.

Off in the distance, somewhere beyond the tall pines, lay CPR harbor. It might as well have been on the moon. I felt very alone and desolate.

Suddenly, I heard a strange noise. I turned toward it, trying to figure out from where it was coming. Somewhere over that rise, beyond the pines, was something that sounded like a chainsaw being started. Then it settled into a burbling note. I could hardly believe my ears.

An outboard engine.

Where there was an outboard, there was a boat. And help.

I grabbed my mike. "*Pan! Pan!*" I yelled. "I am aground near the entryway to CPR Slip, and I need assistance. Particularly from that small boat I just heard starting."

I stuck my head next to the radio speaker. What were the chances that someone had their radio ears on? At this very moment?

A woman's voice answered.

"Can I get some help?" I asked.

"But of course you can!" she announced in her fine Canadian voice. The answer was remarkably unconcerned.

I slumped on the deck, mike in hand, somewhat dazed. I had made contact.

I did not know how I would get off this pile of rocks. But help was on its way.

*   *   *

Around the island's tip roared a small, aluminum runabout. At the tiller was a man in a panama-type hat, its wide brim shielding his face. Beneath his wide smile, he was dressed in colorful shorts and a t-shirt as if he were on an island cruise in the Caribbean. His partner, leaning back on a bow seat, was garbed in shorts and an overly large t-shirt emblazoned with a red maple leaf on it.

"Hey," Greg Richard said, throttling back and staying outside the reefs. "Having a little trouble?"

"Could use a little help," I allowed, wondering what a little fishing boat could do.

Jake Hayton jumped in the cold water, seemingly unconcerned, and splashed over to my stranded boat. In his hand was a heavy line. I wrapped it round my starboard bow cleat.

With Jake shoving my boat, Gregg gave the engine some

gas and the 35-h.p. outboard roared. I could feel my boat's keelson and stub keel crunch against rocks.

The boat lurched, moved and took on a surprising lightness. We bobbed up and down, alive again. And in deeper water.

"Thanks," I yelled.

Greg circled around with the runabout to pick Jake up out of the water. They waved and headed off for the harbor entryway.

I got my centerboard down without difficulty. The rudder, though, flopped back and forth in my hand. It had jammed out of its hold-down, which now was bent out of shape. Without the rudder firmly in its gudgeons, I'd lose control.

I dashed below, grabbed a length of braided line and looped it over the aft section of the tiller, near the rudder head. I added a few loops through a rear teak handhold on the transom and tightened the line with some quick half-hitch knots.

I wiggled the rudder back and forth. Not too elegant, but it worked. I had steering again.

To the north of me, well beyond a point of land, my jaunty Canadian friends were in animated conversation. But they were waiting for me.

I started the Nissan and motored slowly toward them.

They saw me coming and picked up speed. I followed them carefully.

I had discovered all the rocks I wanted to today.

*   *   *

My Canadian friends were careful to stay fairly close to the spit of L-shaped land. There was a narrow channel that began close to the shore, dropping off quickly. I followed them around a rocky point.

CPR harbor opened up to me. To the west, St. Ignance Island's green hills protected it; to the north and the east rose a hillock, heavily covered with pines. I saw a few boats, including a large steel cruiser carrying the Canadian flag. It was the Ogima II.

My Canadian friends waved goodbye and headed to the beach beside *Ogima*. At the end of one dock, a Canadian boater motioned to me and helped me come in. I put down fenders and threw him my dock lines. I was secure.

I felt the sunshine beam down on my face; I looked up at the beautiful blue skies, lined with a few cotton-candy clouds. In this all-weather harbor, I felt only the mildest of breezes; the hills protected me. What a beautiful place.[3]

A sudden thought crossed my mind. What had happened to *Persistence's* centerboard trunk during the grounding? We had plowed into the rocks at a slow speed, but had gotten caught on the tip of the centerboard and the rudder. When we came out of the rocks, I heard crunching and scraping noises under the hull.

I pulled up the starboard floorboards — water! Damn.

I ran my flashlight over the join between the hull and the keelson. There was a puddle of water, but I couldn't feel anything broken. I felt upward with my fingers to the big bronze bolt holding the centerboard in place. No jagged pieces or splinters of wood.

Hauling out my dishwashing pan and my boat sponge, I mopped up the water. There wasn't a lot. I guessed I had taken a couple of quarts.

I brought out a cloth towel and wiped the bilge area until it was dry.

I waited a bit, watching to see what would happen. I lay on the floorboards and began to sweat. I realized it was not the stress.

It was warm in beautiful CPR Harbor. The Canadians who came out to rescue me had been dressed as if they were on a Caribbean cruise. In my long underwear, polar fleece and wool socks, I was mightily overdressed.

I was thinking I should change clothing when I again reached into the bilge.

My finger felt that chill of water.

We were leaking!

I played my flashlight down into the area. Little beads of water were oozing in near the trunk. Not a lot of water, but distressing. I realized that only three-eighths-inch of wood, now cracked or broken, separated me from the bottom of the harbor.

I swabbed the bilge out both with a sponge and a towel, and when I was done, felt with my fingers that the bilge was dry.

I waited. A few minutes later there was seepage, but it seemed to be less. The leak seemed to be decreasing.

My beautiful wooden boat was healing itself. The wood was swelling shut, just like wood always does. If I were really lucky, maybe it'd take care of itself.

I stuffed my sponge and towel into the bilges. I'd come back in a short time and check.

In the meantime, I knew I'd still have a boat under me. I just hoped the floorboards would not be floating when I returned.

*   *   *

It was time to properly pay my respects to the rescuers and to meet the lady who had answered my distress call.

I walked down the beach to *Ogima,* a sturdy-looking, 40-foot steel motor cruiser, where I was welcomed aboard. Here I again met my rescuers, Jake Hayton, who had plunged into the chill water to shove my boat off, and the jaunty skipper of the runabout, Gregg Richard. I also met the large golden lab Maggie, who was the ship's dog.

I recognized Lynda Blanchette when she spoke. It was her fine Canadian voice that consoled me on the airwaves when I went aground. Lynda co-owned the *Ogima* with Gregg.

Jake and his friend Marie Cowley, both of Thunder Bay, were onboard as passengers and were friends with Gregg and Lynda.

"We talked to the Coast Guard," Lynda told me. "They heard your distress call, and we told them you were lightly aground, and that we were going out to assist you."

"Thank you," I said. "I appreciated the help more than you know. "

"No problem," she said, smiling brightly. "Cruise Lake Superior and you'll find a few rocks from time to time. Everybody does."

Including me. I smiled appreciatively.

I learned that Gregg and Lynda, long-time Superior boaters, operated the *Ogima* as their own venture during their summers.

They call themselves the Rossport Island Tours, which their literature describes as "A Superior Experience."

I liked this Canadian vessel and her people. Maybe it showed, for in short order, I got invited for a beer, a quick tour of the *Ogima*, and then for lunch. The lunch was excellent, with some of Lynda and Gregg's homemade wine, and the look at *Ogima* was instructive. *Ogima* once was the Abitibi Paper Company's executive vessel on Lake Nipigon[4]. A big white motor cruiser, she has private sleeping rooms, a washroom, a dining center, a large pilothouse well equipped with navigation equipment, and is powered by a new 200-h.p. diesel engine. Her home port is Rossport[5], where I was headed.

Much refreshed, I walked back along the shore, cocking my head to the weather. It was a pleasant, sunny day, with little breeze here in the harbor. The pines gave off their fragrance above the lake-swept air.

Nearing my boat, I tensed up as I looked carefully at her waterline. She was on her marks; no, we weren't sinking.

Inside, I rummaged my way to the starboard floorboard and laid down. I probed the varnished bilge with my fingers. No water! I lifted out the sponge and the towels. They were wet after absorbing the seepage. But they had contained the leak. It seemed to be slowing.

My luck was holding.

*   *   *

"We're off to Agate Island," Lynda hollered over at me. "Want to come?"

"Sure," I said, and we piled into the 16-foot runabout and soon were zooming out of the entrance and out onto the lake.

I glanced out to see some flagged markers for several reefs I had not noticed earlier.

There were also a couple of other reefs I could make out in the clear water. This area was not the easiest one to get in and out of, unless you knew what you were doing. But in the shallow-draft outboard, we could skim along the surface with no problems.

"Are there actually agates here?" I asked.

"Why do you think they call it Agate Island?" Lynda grinned.

On the western shore of the island, Gregg ran the runabout up on the gravel beach, and we hopped out. Lynda and Gregg showed us how to look for agates along the beach.

"Here," she said, holding up a lovely rock with a purple part to it. "An agate." Moments later, we were all bent over, scrutinizing the pebbles in the water and in the gravel. Yes, I found one and washed it off.

It was like a child's scavenger hunt, with the reward being agates that you found yourself. But I was not nearly as good as Lynda, who ended up giving me several of her treasures.

On the island, the sun burned down, accompanied by a light breeze. There was a heaviness in the air, making the heat a little more intense than usual.

The wind had come up while we were agate hunting and we had a choppy ride back that splashed foam on me. I had my nylon jacket zipped up under my PFD, and so the cold water really didn't bother me too much.

But it was amazing how quickly, even unnoticed by us, the wind had changed. The flags on the reef markers were standing sideways, and the staffs holding them up were bending like willow branches in the wind. On one reef, the water slashed ominously.

"Getting back just in time," Linda observed.

The beautiful, bright-finished wooden sailboat, *Orenda*, lies at anchor.

Chapter Nineteen

RAINY DAY
IN HARBOR

*What lies behind us and what lies before us
are tiny matters compared to what lies within us.*
—Ralph Waldo Emerson

A s I AWAKENED, I realized two things. I hurt a lot from scrambling around the boat yesterday when I went aground, and secondly, I wasn't going anywhere today.

My clue was a patter on the roof. As I glanced out a portlight, I saw rain slapping at the water, making little holes; the pines had turned black. To the west, St. Ignance Island was a dark, ominous mass with blue-black clouds overhanging it.

I rubbed my eyes and made a tough decision. Today would

not be a good day to fix the rudder or to do any other work in the cockpit. That done, I snapped on my VHF radio, and from 26 feet above me, *Persistence's* antenna speared the airwaves and brought me the weather forecast.

Small craft warning. Thunderstorms. Fog. Moderate to strong southwest winds.

Not too encouraging. I snapped the radio off, muttering once again that I really should have a cup of strong coffee before checking the weather radio.

In my long underwear, wool socks, and polar fleece, I was still cold. My ankle ached.

But soon the espresso burbled, the steam rose, and wonderful aromas engulfed my cabin, along with warmth. My little stove burned like a blowtorch, and in minutes I stopped shivering. Soon I began to feel warm and almost civilized.

The general euphoria lasted long enough for me to lift the floorboards and feel around with my fingers. Yeah, it was down there all right. I shone my Maglite down into the bilges. It was glistening — a goodly puddle.

The lake was making its way in from somewhere. Maybe I had cracked the keel or the centerboard trunk when I went aground yesterday. I remembered that we had been bouncing up and down, and the keel had hit with a sickening bump, bump.

As I mopped up the water, I had the ominous feeling that I was scraping through these adventures by the skin of my teeth — using up my luck.

One of these times I wouldn't be so lucky.

*   *   *

The caffeine was kicking in and I felt a little jittery. What would I have to eat? On this cold, wet morning, maybe a couple of eggs over easy, along with a rasher of bacon, might taste good. Some toasted English muffins, coated with good Canadian jam?

My mouth watering, I began to rummage about the bilges.

No eggs, of course, much less muffins and bacon. The bilges nevertheless produced a damp-looking sealed packet of lowfat grain cereal with dehydrated fruit. Just heat up a little water, fill up the cup — and voila! Hearty breakfast.

I ended up with a sort of half-cooked grain cereal with tough, dry fruit. Not quite that rasher of bacon and eggs of which I dreamed, but a small voice echoed piously, "... so much better for you, too."

As I ate, I had the wooden hatch open, with the rain kept out by my home-made dodger. This little patch of green cloth and plastic provided the cabin below with a prism of light, illuminating it and me. The dodger was a little steeple, not unlike that of a church, pulling in brightness and cheering me.

Breakfast finished, I did some routine clean-ups in the cabin. I moved some soggy clothing around. I checked my two marine batteries with my voltmeter. These were located below my bunk, securely strapped to the keelson. They not only provided me with power for my radios, instruments, and lighting, they formed part of my ballast weight down below. Both had a full charge. The photovoltaic cells on my cabin top were keeping them topped up.

I did my "to do" list. I'd have to fix the tiller and refill the main gas tank. I'd also noted I was running low on drinking water. I got out my charts and selected my route through the islands to Rossport. I carefully wrote down key GPS positions on the chart and entered these landmarks in my Magellan.

I had to be ready to go once the fog and storms let up.

*　*　*

I put on my foul weather gear and clambered off the boat. I'd stretch my aching muscles and take another look at where I had gone aground on the rocks. It still bothered me that I had made such an error.

I sauntered into dark woods overhung with moss and found a pine-laden trail. I hobbled over a rise — and stopped and stared. Before me was something like a vision come true.

Anchored off the reefs, bobbing lightly in the mists, was a wooden sailboat — a golden beauty. She was bright finished, and her tall wooden mast gleamed under many coats of varnish.

My eyes took in the sweep of her sheer, looking at the carefully matched mahogany planking and the inset portlights. My heart leapt out to her. In many ways, she reminded me of my own Persistence, grown, somehow magically, bigger. A lot bigger.

"Ahoy, the wooden boat," I hailed. I saw a sailor come out and move about on the deck. He looked up, surprised to see a lone stranger emerging from the woods.

I learned the boat was the *Orenda*, owned by Michael Keyser of Calgary, and I was invited aboard. "We'll come to get you," he said, and soon, a small inflatable glided toward me, rowed by Mike. He was accompanied by crew member, Cam Reid.

We paddled out the entryway. As we came closer, *Orenda* seemed to grow bigger and more massive. I reached out to touch the glowing wood.[1] It was smooth and the finish deep, like a musical instrument. "Just varnish," Mike explained, "no epoxy on top."

I liked it. Mike kept rowing the little inflatable and gave me a water-line tour of the great wind ship. The woodwork was gorgeous. At the stern, he stopped.

"Come aboard," Mike said, taking hold of the rudder. The stern section loomed above me, and I looked for a ladder or some steps.

"Here's how we do it," Cam said. As Mike steadied the inflatable, Cam stood up and grasped the rudder blade. He'd put his left foot on a massive gudgeon and stepped out of the dinghy. He hauled himself upward, placing his hands on a handle midway up the rudder. Another step and he swung himself over the transom.

He leaned out, smiling. "Your turn," he said.

Mike braced the inflatable as I inserted my foot atop the gudgeon — it seemed to fit OK. A step was bolted onto the rudder stock, with handholds. I lifted upward, now dangling in space.

"Here," Cam showed me another handhold, and I lunged for it.

Moments later, I was aboard. My eyes traveled up the 65-foot mast, laminated of golden Sitka spruce, the varnished wood shining brightly. Here was a boat anyone could love.

"*Orenda*," Mike explained as he joined us, "is a word from the Huron Indians. When they sat around a campfire, they prayed for orenda — positive energy." I was getting just that.

I learned that *Orenda* is a Vic Carpenter boat, 45 feet length overall, and a sister ship to Golden Goose, which the legendary Canadian shipbuilder crafted for singer-songwriter Gordon Lightfoot. Lightfoot's mournful Superior dirge plays every November 10 — *The Wreck of the Edmund Fitzgerald.*[2] I'd read about Carpenter in *WoodenBoat*[3] magazine, in which the publication told of his extreme dedication to woodwork, and of the efforts of his wife, who does the varnishing. A Carpenter ship was a masterpiece in wood. And here I was on one.

Mike and Cam unzipped the cloth cover off the helmsman's wheel. It was hand-crafted of alternating strips of mahogany and Sitka spruce, and flawlessly varnished. I grasped the five-foot diameter wheel and turned it from side to side. The wheel was precise and powerful, and even at anchor, the boat felt alive, almost ready to fly away.

"It's a wonderful wheel," Mike said, "Never cold or wet or slippery."

Mike slid back the entry hatch, and instinctively, I slipped out of my boat mocs and reverently trod down the wooden steps in my heavy wool socks.

"Wish I could get my crew to do that," Mike observed. Cam seemed not to notice.

It was like stepping inside a piece of sculpture. Wood flowed with sensuous curves. Bunks seemed to grow out of the Western Red Cedar hull. Overhead handrails were sculptured to the cabin top. The ship's ribs glowed in their assembly of mahogany laminates.

It was a woodworker's dream. Everything was beautifully finished so all the wood showed.

I stopped under a sparkling jewel of light. It was a deck prism, the old-fashioned kind that the old sailing ships used to

Photo / Cam Reid

The author at the helm of *Orenda*. Note the custom-built wooden wheel.

bring in light. In the bow area, a massive bunk rose from the wooden deck, its sides all sculpted in wood. This was the skipper's stateroom. In the stern was the navigator's salon, a big one in varnished wood and full of natural light, thanks to an overhead hatch and portlights. The working table was big enough to open up a large nautical chart.

Orenda used to race, I learned. "Carpenter (her builder) took her to the Mackinac races for about ten years and the Trans-Superior once or twice," Mike explained. "She's well balanced at the helm in all points of sail, and my wife, Judy, and I have sailed her to windward in 40 knots of wind. She's a strong boat."

Mike and Cam had sailed out of Canada's Georgian Bay through the North Channel and came through the locks at Sault Ste. Marie to CPR Slip, a distance of about 500 miles so far. This was a traveling machine. For her to cover so much ground so fast meant she was quick.

As we prepared to depart, I slipped behind the wheel again and tried to imagine what it would be like to drive 1,200 square feet of sail piled on that golden mast. "She handles like a dinghy," Mike assured me.

I looked up at the tall mast, a smile on my lips. Yeah.

Getting down the big rudder[4] was no more difficult than climbing up. The tricky part was stepping down into the inflatable, bobbing in the water, but Mike had gone ahead and was bracing it securely. Cam followed, and slowly we rowed back through the entryway.

I turned around to have one more look. *Orenda* had taken on a ghostly hue. Agate Island, off to the east, had already disappeared.

The fog had rolled in and the golden ship was lost in the mist.

*   *   *

I was in the cockpit of my own boat, ready to go below and warm up. Mike and Cam had rowed back to the anchored *Orenda*. I hadn't thought there was anyone else out on the water when out of the mists glided two sea kayaks.

"Can we put in here?" the tall kayaker asked, unsure of himself, as they pulled alongside *Persistence*

"Sure," I said. I had been here less than 24 hours, and I was now the resident expert. I directed them to a grassy knoll just beyond my own boat. "Help yourself."

They were chilled and looked exhausted. As they unpacked their gear for the night, overturning their kayaks, the full story came out. They had been in the winds yesterday, but finally put ashore. In a kayak, they could simply pull off and wait it out. "But we like sandy beaches, not rocky ones like we've been having," explained one. "Rock beds are hard to sleep on."

The tall man, I learned, was a forester, and the smaller kayaker was a cardiologist.

"And you are a writer," said the small man. I was surprised. I had not mentioned my profession.

"Yeah," I admitted. "Actually, an author."

"I knew it," said the forester with a grin. He explained: "There are predominately two occupations here on the lake: photographers and writers."

"A lot of them?" I was surprised.

"Oh, sure. We've already run into several of them. One guy only photographs sunrises."

"No sunsets?"

"Only sunrises. He claims they're different. He's doing a book."

The kayakers had been making their way east through the islands, paddling all day long. "On a good day, we make maybe 30 miles," the forester explained. "Kayaks are really an easy way to go camping. You've got all your gear in the boat and you're just sliding along."

"Like the voyageurs?"

"Oh, no, that was different. They did many more miles a day and they did it hard."

"I find it difficult to imagine anyone out on that lake in a canoe. Or a kayak."

"A kayak is close to the water," the forester explained, surprised. "It makes you very stable. When you put your cockpit skirt on, you are tolerably water tight."

"Do you carry a radio?" I asked, thinking of the VHF weather reports from Environment Canada that I listened to so carefully.

"No," they said. "We watch the water. When it gets rough, we pull off. So why do we need a radio?"

"You don't check the forecasts?"

"We see what's coming."

"I still think you guys are a lot like the old voyageurs."

"I can't imagine anyone out on the lake in an open canoe." Shaking their heads, they looked over at *Persistence*. A gleam came into the foresters' eyes. "Or in a sailboat like yours."

What? Each to his own, I thought.

One kayaker carefully stepped aboard *Persistence*. He tentatively stood upright in on a cockpit seat, then jiggled up and down. As the little sailboat rocked a little from side to side, a contrived look came over his face.

With an exaggerated gesture, and holding his stomach, he quickly stepped off.

"I'm seasick already," he announced.

I grinned. But I realized he was only partially joking.

*   *   *

Ed and Doreen DeWilde, of Seymour, Wisconsin, had the dock next to me and also were fogbound — going nowhere today. Like me, they had come up to the lake at the wrong time.

"We seemed to be following the storm," Ed told me as he leaned back on his power boat, *The Wild Thing*, a 25-foot, 260-h.p. vessel built along the lines of a cigarette boat with a cabin. Ed is a welding instructor at Northeast Wisconsin Technical College in Green Bay.

As Ed told me about his experiences, I began to learn more about the Independence Day or Green Storm. On July 4, he and his wife were towing the *Wild Thing* behind their car from their home in Seymour for a week's cruise on Superior. First, they dropped their oldest daughter, Rachel, off to catch a flight to Germany at the Minneapolis Saint Paul International Airport. At about 5 p.m., they headed north to Duluth and then northeasterly on Hwy. 61, the road that snakes through the Sawtooth Mountains along the edge of Superior.

"That was an experience, trailering a boat along the North Shore in terrible winds," Ed told me.

"Two Harbors was flooded," Ed said. "Power was out. All along the highway, there were areas where the blacktop was washed out. There were 12-foot troughs on the shore side from water coming down out of the hills. Parts of Hwy. 61 were shut down. In 30 to 40 areas, we had to hug the centerline because the road was washed out on one side. There had been a tremendous amount of rain."

Going further north, they stopped at Grand Marais, Minnesota, where they heard reports of people missing in the "back country," the hard-hit wilderness canoe area.

"The power lines were out; huge trees were down all over," he said.

Not deterred, they continued across the Canadian border into the city of Thunder Bay where they launched their powerboat. Ed's *Wild Thing* could cover a lot of territory with its top speed of 45 m.p.h. and cruising speed of 30 m.p.h. In a few hours, they made it across the bay and to Isle Royale's Windigo Harbor for the night.

Days later, leaving Windigo Harbor, they again ran into trouble. Coming back from the south end of Isle Royale, they started in calm seas, but soon the winds began blowing hard. Ed said, "I never expected seas to intensify like that — and it got worse and worse in the 45-m.p.h. winds."

I nodded. That would have been when I was on the open waters heading from Silver Islet for Loon Harbor.

The *Thing* plunged through five-to six-foot seas as Ed and Doreen punched their way to Thompson Island. It was a rough ride, with water splashing over the boat, but when they approached Thompson they had another problem — finding the harbor.

Ed had picked up his GPS landmark to the island, but could not see the harbor, so he followed Thompson's seaward side to the east — until he came to the three small islands beyond it. "I was getting nervous in the big seas," Ed said, "especially when I saw the seas breaking on the rocks."

Like me, he had overshot the harbor and had gone to the end of the island. He started to go around the tip and through the rough pass, but on a sudden premonition, chanced a look over his left shoulder.

"All of a sudden," he said, "we saw the harbor. It was like a little paradise." He added that "from the south, there was no way to see it. It looks like a natural rock wall."[5]

Ed relaxed a little. "You get respect for this large body of water," he said. "The weather changes so fast. All of a sudden, you have winds out of nowhere."

*   *   *

Fog changed to rain, and somewhere off in the distance thunder rolled.

On the shore near me, the owners of a red inflatable were working on the small craft in the downpour. The boaters were off a large power boat that had arrived yesterday. A sign on their windshield boldly proclaimed: "I'm here on earth to see how much fossil fuel I can burn."

They had been out in their inflatable in the fog yesterday and had to radio for help because they were lost, and their inflatable was losing air. Finally, a boat from the harbor went out to get them.

"Get it fixed?" I asked, helpfully.

"Yeah," said one, not looking up. "The valves."

"What?" I asked, not understanding. It was like that this day. Rain around us; rain fogging the brain.

"The chambers are OK," he said patiently, continuing his work. "The kids just didn't screw down the valves."

I saw that they were re-gluing some patches. Apparently they had learned a lesson yesterday and were checking over their craft.

"Good enough!" one guy said, standing up in the rain. He thumped the inflatable's side. "Let's go fishing."

*   *   *

In my foul weather gear, I wandered in the mists away from the harbor, following a solitary path into the woods. I admired the spruce trees and the gray moss that hung from their branches. It was dark even during the day, with the tree branches crowding out the sky. My boat mocs stepped noiselessly on eons of fallen fir needles.

So unchanged was this primitive island that I could imagine myself stepping back in time. It was quiet, too, save for the murmur of the lake, but sometimes silence is overwhelming.

You ever get this feeling? You know, where you get connected to something you don't understand and can't quite explain? It's there, this familiarity on a deep level within you, maybe something out of a primordial memory.

Here I was, in the north woods primeval, the stuff of which Hiawatha sang, a wilderness to this day. Splendid isolation; beauty all around me.

A sudden, weird thought occurred to me. It was odd that I had not heard any birds or seen sea gulls. Or animals.

As I returned, I saw a group of boaters had gathered around

a communal fire pit. They had a roaring blaze going. Someone remarked: "They've sighted moose on the island — and a timber wolf."

So there was something out there. Maybe it saw me, but I did not see it. Whatever. I decided it was just as well to make my way back to my boat.

*　　*　　*

The sky lowered, and the island grew dark. There was a stillness in the air. I felt the wilderness slipping deep into my soul. There was no moon tonight, no illumination. Just blackness of the kind you don't see in the city.

Even in this island paradise, I was hurting. I lay in my bunk twisting from side to side, trying to get my ankle in the "right" position. I found that if I placed my foot exactly right, the ache would diminish. A little.

I had already taken a good dose of no-aspirin aspirin. Nightcap of champions. But it wasn't knocking down all that ached.

I found I was getting anxious to get on my way, pain or no pain, leak or no leak.

Shaky, I reached over and snapped on Environment Canada. The VHF forecast for tomorrow: security alert — small craft warning.

I shook my head, mindful of what a Thunder Bay boater told me:

"Up here, you have to move or you never go anywhere. If you listen to them, they'll scare the hell out of you."

That seemed to make sense.

Chapter Twenty

A STORM TALE:
THE SOLE SURVIVOR

In a real dark night of the soul,
It is always three o'clock in the morning.
— F. Scott Fitzgerald

IT IS 1:30 A.M. After sleeping only a few hours, I am propped upright in my sleeping bag against the starboard side of my bunk. The chill cabin is bathed in the red glow of the battery panel's tiny bulb. It keeps me company. Below me, water in the bilge is rising.

Things are catching up with me. I cannot sleep. The painkillers aren't working. I am so stiff that at times I think I am going to fall over on my face. Over the sound of the cold waves and the swish of the rising water in the bilge, things whisper to me in the night. What if I'd wrecked my boat? What if I fell overboard and had to survive in the frigid water? Once those waters touched me ...

I took a deep breath. My fears were overreaching my mind.

I focused on the story of another sailor, a man who had survived worse than I could imagine.

*   *   *

Her starboard side lashed by mounting waves, the *S.S. Daniel J. Morrell* clawed northward. It was November 28, 1966, and a hard storm had blasted across Lake Huron. As the long night deepened, the tough old ore boat[1] began to blow around, pitching and rolling in 25-foot-high seas.

By 2 a.m., she had fought her way off the thumb of Michigan's "mitten," known as the graveyard for ships. Confused seas swept her length; she took green water over her bow.[2]

In his forward quarters, able-bodied seaman Dennis Hale was asleep. The 26-year-old, 250-pound Hale, in his third season on the lakes, woke up when books fell off his bookshelf with a loud "bang."

Alarmed, Dennis sat up and tried to click on his bunk light. The bulb stayed dark.

When the emergency bell split the night, sounding the general alarm, Dennis grabbed a life jacket and rushed on deck.

Gusts of wind hit him; he staggered to stand upright. Standing ankle deep in icy slush, clad only in his life jacket and undershorts, he shivered as he peered down the spar deck.

Something was wrong with the boat.

In the center, the steel deck was bending crazily, grinding up and down and groaning as sparks flew from the twisting metal. Like a vent from Hades, steam billowed out.

Suddenly, the deck reared high in the air.

The boat was breaking apart.

Frantic, Dennis dashed back to his cabin to find more clothing, but in the darkness, he could only grab his wool peacoat. He threw that on over his lifejacket and hurried back to the deck.

He felt the snow on his face, the frigid wind on his naked

legs and the ice under his bare toes. Around him the black seas roiled.

*   *   *

Shivering, he climbed aboard the pontoon life raft[3], lashed atop a hold behind the pilot house. It was an open raft, a last-ditch survival floatation unit with no weather protection. Some of the crew were already onboard the raft; some stood alongside. One man lashed himself directly to the raft.

Despite the cold and the working of the ship, everyone was quite calm. They talked confidently among themselves, despite the fact that no Mayday could be sent. The power cables, running from the engine room in the stern to the forward section, had snapped with the breakup of the hull. Dennis tried, without any luck, to mooch a cigarette from a buddy.

The end came quickly.

Dennis saw the one-inch thick steel deck start to tear in half, from one side to another. The gap widened as the aft section slowly separated and fell back. It was still afloat — but at an angle to the bow section.

Lights were still on inside the hull; the aft section glowed yellow. Engine still running, propeller churning, the cavernous section charged forward — the severed hull headed straight toward them.

Danger! Dennis watched it come, clutching a handhold on the raft.

As it neared, he closed his eyes and the next thing he remembered was that it was dark and he was struggling in icy waters, not knowing which way was up.[4]

He had survived a 50-foot fall into heavy seas.

Not far away, the pontoon raft bobbed, its automatic emergency light beckoning to him in the darkness. High waves at times obscured the light, but Dennis kept his bearings and swam hard.

Exhausted and cold, he pulled himself aboard, where he found deckhands Arthur Sojek, 33, and John Cleary Jr., 20. Minutes later, they helped pull wheelman Charles Fossbender from the icy lake.

Only the four men had survived the fall and made it to the raft.

They scanned the seas, and hailed for survivors. No one answered.

In the storage compartment they found flares, a flare gun, and a flashlight. They fired off some of the flares in a desperate attempt to signal any ships in the area. None responded.

Minutes later, Charles Fossbender excitedly waved the flashlight back and forth, "signaling that ship over there."

Dennis shielded his eyes in the spray and driving wind. There was another ship not far away.

He shook his head. It was not a ship to rescue them. A blackness sank into the pit of his stomach.

In the storm, Fossbender had mistaken the *Morrell's* ghostly stern, still brightly lighted and under power, sailing away.

*   *   *

The men were exposed to the driving winds and freezing spray. Soaked and desperate, they could only huddle on the grating between the two pontoons, trying to stay warm.

Most were not dressed better than Dennis. Only Charles Fossbender, who had been on watch, was fully clothed.

By dawn, John Cleary and Art Stojek were dead. Only Dennis and Fossbender were left.

Dennis lay on his left side, his head cradled under one arm, on the partly collapsed storage compartment. Fossbender was behind him, facing away, curled with his legs up. Both men were shivering uncontrollably.

At about 2 p.m., Fossbender raised himself. "I can see land," he said.

"How far away is it?" Dennis asked.

"Quite a distance," Fossbender responded.

But two hours later, Fossbender died.[5]

Dennis was the sole survivor.

And he was freezing to death.

Desperately alone, Dennis thought up ways to stay alive. He tried to move parts of his body even a little bit to keep up circulation.

He put his fingers in his mouth so they would not freeze.

He didn't urinate for fear that the warmth he had in his groin would escape — and he'd die.[6]

The raft ran aground on rocks several hundred feet from shore. Dennis could see lights from a farmhouse. To get help, he fired several flares, holding the broken flare gun together with his bare hands; no one saw them. He yelled hoarsely when he heard the sounds of people.

No one answered.

He tried to move from the raft, but was almost paralyzed by the cold. His unused muscles knotted with cramps.

In pain, he could only lay and watch.

He couldn't give up hope. If he remained where he was, someone would see the raft. They'd come out to rescue him.

Somebody, somewhere would notice that the *Morrell* was missing and they'd send a search party. He nursed himself through the long day with hope.

By nightfall, the wind arose again and cold descended on his numbed body. Breakers rolled over the raft.

Dennis drifted in and out of sleep. Ice coated him.

The next morning, right after dawn, he awoke with a start. He saw the farmhouse lights come on. He yelled and yelled again for help, but no one answered.

It began to snow.

*   *   *

By afternoon, he was ravaged by thirst. Earlier, he had been able to drink a little lake water off the lanyard of his flare gun, but that was gone now.

Ice had formed on his peacoat. Painfully, he managed to move his head about, ready to suck the ice on his coat — when he saw something that stopped him.

Floating above the raft and looking down on him was a man dressed all in white. He had a white mustache and white hair, and nearly translucent, bluish skin. His eyes burned with intensity.

"Don't eat the ice off your pea coat," he commanded in a loud voice. He vanished as mysteriously as he had arrived.

Dennis laid his head back down on the raft, still thirsty. Wind howled across the wave crests, sweeping across his ice-coated body.

He lost track of time. After a while, he felt himself floating, moving upward, as if a force had come up behind him and was sucking him away from the raft. As he rose higher and higher, he felt the pain and the cold receding.

He was headed toward a white light, as if at the end of a tunnel, and when he emerged he saw a green, grassy field, well cut, with a little depression, and a bridge going across it.

A man dressed in white stood waiting. He took Dennis' hands in his and said, "Let us see what you have learned."

Dennis' whole life flashed before him as he answered the man's questions. When he was finished, the man released the sailor's hands and told him that he could pass over.

On the bridge's other side, his mother appeared — a woman he recognized only from pictures. She told him how glad she was to see him at last. Long-dead loved ones and relatives gathered around.

He descended into a mist until he came to the bow of the *Morrell*, lying in a valley. Aboard were all his old shipmates, hugging him and clapping him on the back.

Out of the mist glided the stern section of the *Morrell*. It joined up with the forward section almost seamlessly. Dennis and his shipmates rushed to it and clambered down below, where they found the rest of the crew at work. They talked excitedly about how glad they were to be together again.

The third engineer, George Dahl, came up a ladder and stared at Dennis. "What are you doing here?" he asked. "It's not your time." All conversation stopped. Someone said, "You've got to go back," and Dennis found himself being lifted again, hoisted into the whirlwind.

He was back on the raft, all alone. His thirst had returned. He began to bite at ice when the man in white again appeared overhead.

He shook a finger at Dennis. "I told you not to eat the ice off your peacoat," he warned. "It'll lower your body temperature, and you'll die." Dennis stopped eating ice.

*   *   *

In the offices of the Bethlehem Steel fleet, the chief dispatcher became worried. The reporting station at the locks at Sault Ste. Marie had not reported the Morrell's arrival, nor that of the Townsend, also out in the gale. On Wednesday morning, he called the Coast Guard, which located the Townsend anchored in the St. Mary's river. Where was the *Morrell*?

At 1:12 p.m. Wednesday, a body was sighted at Harbor Beach. When the Coast Guard recovered it, they saw the man wore a life jacket with the *Morrell's* name on it. The Coast Guard broadcast an alert.

An hour later, a freighter saw wreckage about four miles north-northeast of Harbor Beach. It picked up ring buoys and an oil can with the Morrell's name on it. At 2 p.m., it recovered three bodies.

They searched the snow-covered shoreline until late in the afternoon when a helicopter crew saw a life raft near the shore. In it, coated with ice, were four bodies.

As they descended, one of them raised his hand, waving feebly. It was Dennis.

*   *   *

The helicopter landed on its pontoons in the shallow, choppy water. Crewmen splashed out, wading toward the raft. They had to roll the half-frozen man off.

At Harbor Beach, an ambulance rushed Dennis to the hospital. He had lost some skin from his hands, and there was frostbite on his left foot. His skin hadn't turned black, but his body temperature hovered at 94 degrees — dangerously below normal. They packed anything that would hold warm water around his body to raise his temperature.[7]

Out on Huron, boats criss-crossed the lake to fish out bodies. Of the Morrell's 29-man crew, they recovered only twenty frozen corpses. Eight men are still missing.

Only one man returned alive.

*   *   *

When I met him at a lecture held at the Minnesota State

Historical Society's building in Saint Paul, Dennis had a limp and moved down stairs hesitantly. A big man, well over six feet, he is in his 60s, with silver hair, and is the curator of the Ashtabula Great Lakes Marine and U.S. Coast Guard Memorial in Ashtabula, Ohio.

So much of what I had read and watched on news reports came alive as he recalled the events of the sinking and his own remarkable survival. I watched fascinated as he showed a video program shot by divers on the remains of the *Morrell*[8], lying in about 200 feet of water.

After decades of silence, he finally was able to talk openly about the tragedy that had traumatized him. Though much of his survival story was reported in the media, it only has been in recent years that he could talk about "Doc," the man in white who visited him when he was on the raft, and his remarkable "out-of-body" experiences.

He noted that the shipping line did not notify the Coast Guard of its overdue vessel until a day and a half after the sinking, when the first body was found. "That was just four hours before they picked me up," he said.

He felt that all shipwrecks should be scrutinized openly, and reasons behind the sinkings found.

One reason for the *Morrell's* breakup was "brittle steel," he said. He noted that when a piece of the *Morrell's* hull was subjected to stress tests, its steel, designed with metal rated for 60,000 pounds per square inch, tested fine when it was checked out at normal temperatures of 60 to 70 degrees. But when the temperature dropped to 35 to 40 degrees, the steel failed at 15,000 pounds per square inch.[9]

"So it was actually brittle when cold," Dennis said. The *Morrell* was made of the same type of steel as another ship — the *Titanic*.

As I walked from the lecture hall, I felt that Dennis had given all sailors a gift. And that is the knowledge we can survive far longer in those waters than anyone had ever thought possible.

He had.

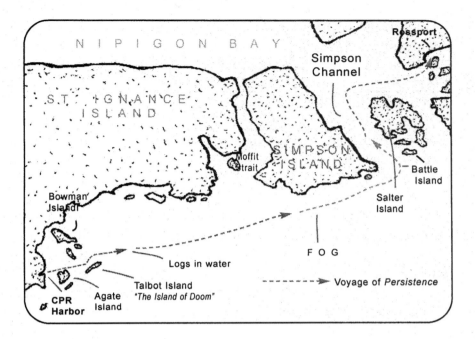

Rossport

Simpson
Channel

S T . I G N A C E
I S L A N D

S I M P S O N   I S L A N D

Moffit
Strait

Battle
Island

Salter
Island

Bowman
Island

FOG

Logs in water

Talbot Island
"The Island of Doom"

CPR
Harbor

Agate
Island

- - - - - - - - ➤ Voyage of *Persistence*

Chapter Twenty One

LOST
IN THE
FOG

*She knows she bears a soul that dares
And loves the dark, rough sea;
More sail! I cry, let her fly;
This is the hour for me.*
— sailing poem

7:30 A.M. FOG WISPED around the harbor; the nearby hills were wreathed in the gray stuff. The air was calm: my flag drooped limply. Water idly lapped at my hull.

I waited patiently.

By 8:30 a.m., fog patches were rolling in and out, like swatches of gray cotton candy, and hid the other islands.

But it was moving.

An hour later I could make out the nearby islands.

"I'm going!" I said as I untied from the dock. The fog was burning off.

I was the first boat out of the harbor, keeping plenty of distance between me and the reefs I had discovered on my way in. I swung north around Agate Island, and headed southeast toward Talbot Island. I'd be on an inside channel — for a while.

As I sailed past Talbot Island, I gave it a wide berth. It seemed to be just another rocky island out here in the middle of nowhere. But I knew it had a dark history.

To the south were wicked reefs that stretched underwater well offshore — dangerous enough so that the Canadian government built Superior's first lighthouse here.

This was the Island of Doom.

I trained my binoculars on the wind-swept chunk of rock. It was desolate-looking, especially today. I couldn't make out a sign of a lighthouse, or even the rocky base where one might have stood. But the island was low; storms could easily have overrun the island and dashed all signs of man away.

*   *   *

Built in 1867, the first lighthouse was a white, wooden tower, illuminated by three kerosene lamps and kept by a man named Perry. In his isolated post on the lonely island, the first lighthouse keeper on Superior was pretty much on his own — including finding his way back to civilization.

At the end of the first season, around mid-December, Perry closed the station and began a voyage in a small sailboat to a trading post at the Nipigon River's mouth. He never made it.

His body was discovered the next spring on a beach beside his overturned boat.

He was victim number one. The next year, the lighthouse was enlarged so the keeper could stay on the island all winter. Captain Thomas Lamphier, a veteran skipper of a Hudson's Bay schooner for nearly 20 years, was hired as keeper and left on the island with his wife.

After the lake froze over late in the fall, he died, leaving his grieving wife isolated on the island with no way of getting help. Since Talbot is largely rock, she had no way of burying her husband. She did the only thing she could; she wrapped Capt. Lamphier in canvas and set her beloved husband a short distance behind the lighthouse in a rock crevasse. All winter long, she lived on the isolated island with her husband's unburied corpse nearby.

It wasn't until the following spring that a group of Ojibway paddlers saw Mrs. Lamphier's urgent signals. They took the body by canoe to Bowman Island[1], where they buried it. Atop his grave, they placed a small cross.

When the lighthouse service ship finally arrived on Talbot Island, the crew almost did not recognize Mrs. Lamphier. Her black hair had turned a ghastly white.

Tragedy also struck the third keeper, Andrew Hynes. At season's end in 1872, Hynes boarded up the lighthouse and set sail in a small boat for Fort William. At the beginning of the voyage, the weather was clear, but a storm suddenly erupted. Winds swept Superior, waves grew, and the temperature plummeted. For 18 days, Hynes fought the inland seas in his open craft. He got as far as Silver Islet, about 60 miles to the west. At the small mining community, the half-frozen keeper lifted himself partway from his boat, told his name and a little of his horrifying voyage. Then he died.

There was no fourth keeper for the island of doom. The government abandoned the lighthouse in 1873 — its macabre record unrivalled by any other Superior lighthouse.

The tower remained standing for years, but legends grew. It was said that when the fog rolled in, someone or something would beat against its wooden sides to warn those still out on the lake. Some saw a ghostly figure of a woman with long white hair, wandering disconsolately about the island.[2]

*   *   *

Ahead lay 16 miles of open water. I sat back in my inside steering seat, slumping a bit. I had my remote control in my hand, with my automatic helm doing all the steering work, and checked my course on my GPS.

Let the boat do the work, I thought to myself. That's how I designed her. Something dark rushed toward us in the water.

I threw the boat to one side and narrowly avoided it. The next one hit the hull with a resounding thump. It was an eternity before it cleared the spinning prop. Had it hit, I might have lost the motor.

I hauled myself out of my comfy little closure, stood up, and squinted. Ahead of the bow and stretching into the horizon were many little black things —- bits of tree stumps, branches, and even logs.

This was the first time I'd come across any debris in the water. From where had all the logs and breakage had come?

I slowed the engine to work our way through the wood pack. I had my hand firmly on the tiller, zigging and zagging.

"Position ... what is your position?" the radio crackled. I did not know who was calling me, or even if it was for me, but I couldn't get to the radio.

All my attention was on my game of dodgem.

This went on for miles. By the time I got past Moffitt strait, the water seemed to clear up. We had passed through the debris field

I quickly checked below. Lifting the floorboards, I could not see any water coming in. My cedar hull had held up, but I did not know how impact resistant the three-eighths-inch cedar would be.

And I'd rather not find out.

*   *   *

The wind started to blow from the southeast and the boat slowed and swayed with the gusts, creaking, groaning, and clanging. The waves were hitting us off our starboard bow, giving us nasty little shoves and splashing some of their white caps aboard.

I glanced below just in time to see a little slop of water shooting up through the open centerboard trunk.

A chill settled in my stomach. I had barely entered the open waters and already I was having problems.

I double-checked my chart, bringing out my dividers. I was on a course of 102 degrees, heading mostly easterly, doing 5.9 m.p.h. I had just changed from a heading of 92 degrees off Grebe Point, trying to avoid a big pile of reefs off Beetle Point.

There was hope. An hour of this and I'd be heading into Simpson Strait, on my way to Lake Nipigon. I'd be in the protection of the islands — and off the open waters of the lake.

I was just putting down my chart and congratulating myself when a white bank rolled in with the wind. All my landmarks disappeared.

Total fog. I could barely see beyond my bow.

My adrenalin surged again. A small voice inside my head warned:

Danger! You should get the heck out of here.

I shook my head, trying to center myself. Sailing Superior is as much a mind game as physical. You have to keep a psychological advantage — and not give in to fear.

I knew I had to concentrate.

Now ... where was that bloody channel?

Not far ahead were the reefs off Simpson Island. It was one thing to look for them when you could see and another to continue in their general direction blindly.

But if I went too far, I'd run across more reefs off Battle Island.

In the inside driving position, I again spread out my chart and worked my dividers. The bouncing ride was not helping. The sweat was dripping down from my face. Having my eyeglasses fog up was not helping either.

I calculated positions and punched in additional landmarks; one to a point directly south of the channel, and some more directly up the channel's mid-point. I hoped I got the numbers right.

In a shaky hand, I wrote the positions on the side of my chart. I nearly stabbed myself with the dividers.

OK, now I had it. The exact point I should steer to was landmark Morn 1, opposite Morn Point. Once this landmark came up, I would make my turn, avoiding the reefs off Morn and also off Battle Island, and head northwesterly to a landmark I dubbed Ch. (channel) 1. Ch. 2 followed, along with coordinates.

Nervously, I settled back, peering out the plastic curtains. But all I could see was the bow of my boat, plunging along, occasionally slinging up spray. The rest was fog and matching water.

I braced myself as the boat rolled about in the waves, one side, then the other. The chart, which I had folded in quarters, swung back and forth from its holder like a pendulum. The GPS was to the right of my nose; I could not miss it. The clock, with its oversize analog hands, was to my left, and I could keep track of time running for dead reckoning. Ahead of me were two compasses, which did not totally agree.

I knew that if I miscalculated, I'd probably be on the rocks before I could see them. I might not have time to turn.

It was past noon, but I had no appetite for food. My stomach was knotted up.

I didn't imagine there would be anyone else dumb enough to be running out here in the fog with me. Still, it was wise to check.

"Security ... security," I broadcast on my VHF radio, identifying myself to the Coast Guard. "I am nearing the south entrance to the Simpson channel, encountering heavy fog and want to contact any boats in the vicinity."

Only static greeted me. I broadcast my security message several more times.

A voice came through the speaker: "We are sending out your warning and your heading." It was the Thunder Bay Coast Guard. They also told me there were a few fishing boats in several coves, but staying put.

Good. I had the channel to myself, so I plugged on, flying low and slow.

My little GPS was giving me speed, heading, and coordinates. It told me how soon I'd get to the next landmark. There were a number of screens I had been using one with an arrow on it telling me if I was on my heading or not.

But where was I exactly? That bothered me. Too close to the edge of the island, and I'd be in some serious rocks. Too far west — more rocks.

Dummy! I almost could have kicked myself, for I realized that I had not used one screen on my GPS — the one that told me *exactly* what my position was, good within about 50 feet. I glanced upward at what must be the heavens and uttered a small thanks.

I clicked on the screen, and there I was. My position. Exactly.

It seemed to me I might be getting a little close to the rocks, so I headed off into the lake a little more. With my dividers, I double-checked the landmark I had selected, then triple checked it. A tense moment. When all the numbers aligned and the stars in the heavens agreed, I punched in my turn. The faithful Autohelm buzzed; the boat turned.

I crossed my fingers for I was navigating on faith. I still couldn't see anything, but I had to be right or I'd run right into the reefs.

I watched the GPS numbers line up. I was, theoretically, west of Battle Island, entering the channel between Simpson Island and Salter Island. After I had hit my landmark, I made another course adjustment to Ch. 1.

The motion of the boat changed. I could feel the difference. The wind and the waves were now coming off my starboard aft quarter.

The day was less gray. Elated, I poked my head out of the flap and looked up. A white orb appeared above me in the gray sky. Below me, the waters turned blue.

The sun was burning the fog away. Miracle of miracles, I was right in the middle of the channel. I could have kissed my little GPS unit. It had guided me safely off the lake.

By 2 p.m., as I neared the north end of Salter Island, a yellow sun beamed overhead; below me, the waters were calm and sparkling.

I was out of the channel and in Nipigon Bay.[3] My God, what a difference! It had turned summer again and I began to per-

From my chart, I knew Barwis Reef lay dead ahead. I slid into the cockpit and pulled out my binoculars to look for the reef marker, but I couldn't see anything. I stood in the cockpit, holding onto the swaying boom, searching the water. According to my chart, there was supposed to be a flashing red light that marked the reefs. No marker.

Out came the chart, the dividers, and the GPS, and I placed them on a towel in the cockpit. I calculated new landmarks to bypass the reef. It was now 3 p.m., and the wind out of the east had slowed my eastward passage to 4.9 m.p.h.

Ahead lay the distinctive round, tree-topped islands of Rossport Harbor. My route was toward Quarry Island, a high, towering island. The sun was beating down on my back, and in all my clothing plus PFD and safety harness, I was perspiring heavily. I felt weary.

And staring directly at a channel marker. Suddenly I realized I was guiding my boat directly toward a red, striped marker.

Reefs!

I yanked the tiller over, correcting my course. I shook my head, realizing that I was not thinking clearly. How stupid could you get? I had nearly put us on the rocks.

We easily rounded the bend and ahead was beautiful Rossport Harbor.

As I came closer to the municipal dock, I blinked twice in the sunlight at the large, white boat tied alongside. It was the *Ogima*. Waving at me was my friend from CPR Slip, Lynda Blanchette.

"Where's the best place to tie up?" I yelled.

She made a motion of her blonde head, as if to say "this way," and walked over to one side. I tossed her my line — and we were inside the L-shaped dock, safe and secure.

"Welcome to Rossport," she said brightly. "Did you have a good trip?"

"A little fog," I allowed.

"You get some of that around here," she said.

Peresistence at the Rossport dock. In the background is Healey Island.

Chapter Twenty Two

COLORFUL ROSSPORT HARBOR

Those who hear not the music think the dancers mad.
—Old saying

OUT IN THE HARBOR, tall islands rose majestically to green roundels carpeted with trees — the most picturesque harbor I had ever seen. The light from the west painted the harbor and islands in a glowing gold, something out of a Turner painting.

I blinked a little, standing in the cockpit as I enjoyed the view and my surroundings. I was secure, bobbing easily at the government dock. Up the hill from me was beautiful, downtown Rossport — population, oh, maybe 100 people. This former fishing village, once a part of the wilderness, was the northernmost hamlet on Superior.

I had the impression of a lot of pine trees up there on the hill and lonesomeness. This was not dispelled by the single gravel road up from the dock that led up a steep hill, past some wood frame houses and into the woods. From the dock, the Old Rossport Inn glowed like a jewel.

This little village would be my home while I stocked up on food and water. I'd been out in the islands for weeks, and frankly I was running low both on provisions and on energy. Fatigue was accumulating and catching up with me. This would be a good place to get the boat and myself shipshape.

I glanced below into the darkened cabin. Big mistake.

The boat was a mess with wet and dirty clothing, gear, supplies, and equipment strewn about, the inevitable result of weeks of on-board living — plus a few touches of heavy weather. Both floorboards were full of soggy clothing and gear, including dirty socks and long underwear; both shelves on both sides of the centerboard were full. A large, damp bath towel was draped across the centerboard trunk itself.

I knew what I had to do first — get the boat back in shape. In the warmth of the afternoon sun, I thought I'd do a leisurely clean-up, including the bilges where I kept my canned goods.

The bilges!

Hurriedly, I pulled up the floorboards and discovered that the port side had water in it. Again. Was this because of the centerboard wracking from when I went on the rocks — or because of the slop that had shot up through the open slot when the fog and the waves rolled in.

Or a combination of both? Whatever, priority one was getting rid of the water. It was sweaty work as I took out the wet canned goods and placed them alongside the centerboard trunk. With a large boat sponge, I mopped up the bilge and then wiped it until it was dry to the touch. I left the floorboards off to help the bilge area dry off.

*   *   *

I was hauling wet gear and clothing out into the cockpit to

dry out when a sailboat came into the dock. I helped them tie up, and we swapped information on the unsettled weather we'd been having. Other boaters gathered around, a little community unto ourselves.

"There's 10 foot swells out there," the boater said, "but no wind."

"You came through the fog?" someone asked.

"Yeah," I answered. "I put out a security call on my radio, but no one was out there."

The boater frowned. "There was another sailboat in the strait with you. You must have just missed them."

*   *   *

A lone sea kayak paddled slowly into harbor, blades flashing in the water, and I recognized the rangy forester from CPR Slip. "Marlin, you made it," he yelled over the water.

He had left in the fog a day earlier from CPR than I had and was now just coming in — minus his sea kayaking companion. "Dropped him off," he said. "I'm going on alone."

"Come in and we'll have a cold beer," I offered.

He thought for a moment, then sadly shook his head. "Can't stop," he said, turning his boat. "I recognized your sailboat and I just wanted to come by and say hello."

"Hello, then," I said. He raised his paddle briefly to answer me and began paddling toward the islands.

I watched him disappear into the distance.

*   *   *

I had hoped to stock up on groceries, juices, bottled water, and maybe even some beer at Rossport. But I learned that the hamlet's sole grocery store had closed years before. There was, however, food — lots of good food — at the inn.

I left my boat tied to the dock and started walking uphill. A turn along the single-lane road led me to the old Rossport Inn, about 50 feet from the railroad tracks. I also would see Ned Basher again.

I'd met Basher some years ago when he'd first opened the Inn and was cleaning out decades of accumulated dirt from the Canadian wilderness and sanding 100-year-old maple floors.

The inn had been built as a hotel in 1884 by the Canadian Pacific Railroad.

When Basher had been a fighter pilot, he'd flown over Rossport and fell in love with the harbor. He eventually bought the inn and began restoring it. As I entered, I marveled at the job he'd done. Varnished golden wooden floors creaked under my feet; there was beautiful wood everywhere, in the reception desk, the wooden staircase, and vaulted ceilings. From somewhere, a radio monitored marine transmissions.

Before I had something to eat, I located Ned, and we began reminiscing. He'd come a long way. "When I first bought this place," Ned said, "I told people I bought a small hotel in a dead end street in a town of 100 people that had been closed for four years. If you run it through a computer, it doesn't look too hot."

I nodded. He added, "But considering that, it has been a very good business."

I could see his restaurant was busy. In addition to his inn's guests, tourists had driven down from the Queen's Highway, atop the hills. Several boaters had wandered up from the Rossport docks.

When I told Ned I was out cruising the islands this summer, he beamed. An avid boater, he's also cruised the Canadian north shore. "The archipelago of islands is the finest cruising on Superior," he said. "It's a trip you can make a number of times and not stay in the same place twice. There's a lot of wilderness and good harbors."

He compared this Canadian area and the Apostle Islands National Lakeshore[1] off Wisconsin's northern border, pointing out that the Apostle Islands have no natural harbors. "If the wind switches, you're in a bad spot. Up here, the islands have inlets, natural harbors, where you can get a good night's sleep. In the Apostles, you'll hit the bow before the keel. Here you need to keep up on your navigational skills because of the rocks and shoals. In the Apostles, there's a lot of boats; here, in many areas, you'll pull in for a night and find yourself all alone."

"If you want to get here, you'll get here," Ned said. "This is still the area for the explorer."

*   *   *

As I walked back to my boat, I saw someone aboard a large trimaran that occupied one end of the dock. I introduced myself to the sailor and learned that he worked at Terrace Bay, about 20 kilometers down the Queens Highway to the east, but lived aboard the 46-foot, three-hulled sailboat.

"I always wanted a nice, large boat, and this was one I could afford," he explained. A home builder had spent years constructing the 46-foot Piver[2] trimaran but had finally sold her.

Last Saturday, he was putting into harbor when the wind had picked up. He encountered rain — and something else.

"*Hail!*" he said, touching his head in amazement. " It was hailing in July!"

*   *   *

A familiar-looking sailboat came chugging into the harbor, flags flying gaily. It was the *Barb*, the 25-foot Albin out of Silver Islet, with my old friend Captain Jim Coslett and his two friends from Thunder Bay, Kevin Kennedy, a fireman, and Michael Kennedy, his brother.

"Hello," I yelled as they came alongside the dock. I was delighted to see them, and I learned they had been exploring the islands around CPR Slip.

There was a mystery to solve. One night, when I was tied along the dock at Silver Islet, heard the sound of a diesel engine and I saw the *Barb* moving smartly out of the harbor. "You had lights up and down your mast and all flags flying. You blew your horn a lot."

I shrugged my shoulders as if to ask why.

"Boat needed exercising," Jim said. A bit of north woods' humor. Later, I heard that Kevin's wife had a birthday. Jim and Kevin had gone out into the harbor to salute her with their self-styled one-boat parade. Perhaps well-lubricated salutes, I guessed.

That evening, we met for supper at the Rossport Inn. Our meal finished, we descended the wooden steps behind the old railroad building. It was a dark night, and walking down a hill, the sounds of a bubbling stream drew closer. I peered into the night: a wooden, Finnish-type sauna nestled beside a brook.

By the light of a kerosene lantern, we stripped off our clothing and climbed to the top of the sauna seats. Beads of sweat formed on my naked body; Kevin ladled water on hot coals. Steam sizzled. I sat dripping with perspiration and heat. It felt good. I was getting into this Canadian fascination with saunas.

"Time to cool off," Kevin announced, and went out the door into the night. I saw the Thunder Bay fire captain splashing, rather energetically, beneath an outdoor shower. "Not bad," he said between clenched teeth, and inquired: "Next?"

I noticed he had no takers. Cautiously, I held my hand under the shower and I understood why: freezing cold. Lightning flashed overhead. Thunder rumbled and a few drops of rain fell. It didn't matter to the four naked guys on the deck. "A little natural lighting," someone joked. For me, it was a natural shower — and a warm one.

At midnight, Jim and I walked slowly down the winding road leading back to the harbor. With no streetlights, the little hamlet of Rossport was black with the night. We could see the beacon at the end of the government dock flashing green.

"Storm's coming in," I said.

"Still coming," the old sailor replied, barely glancing at the lightning-filled skies. The wind was beginning to blow as we walked out on the dock.

"Have to get back," he replied. The *Barb*, tied at the end of the dock, was already starting her dance with the waves.

I turned to my own boat. Little *Persistence* was bobbing in the growing winds. I double checked my dock lines to be certain they were secure for the coming storm, and then I clambered aboard, shutting the hatch behind me.

I settled in for the night, clean and comfortable. I didn't even bother with any pain-killers.

Sometime later that night, the storm hit but I don't remember much about it.

Photo / K. E. Thro Collection & Lake Superior Marine Museum Assn.

Sleek bow high in the air, the *Gunilda* lies hard aground on McGarvey Shoal

Chapter Twenty Three

WRECK
OF THE
GUNILDA

There is, one knows not what sweet mystery about this sea,
whose gently awful stirrings seem to speak of some hidden soul beneath.
—Herman Melville

IT WAS GOOD TO BE UNDERWAY. By 8:30 a.m., my bow was cutting through the blue waters of Rossport harbor, swinging wide to the west around the green peak of Quarry Island and then heading eastward between Healey and Channel islands.

I was on the last part of my voyage into one of the most spectacular island chains in this, the largest island archipelago on the Great Lakes.

It was a perfect day to be out on the water. Soon I was in the Schreiber Channel. My piloting directions told me to be watchful of McGarvey Shoal, which at best is covered with several feet of water. It lays about a half mile north of the west end of

Copper Island, to the south of the center of the channel.

I could not see the reef from my cockpit, but I knew McGarvey Shoal could reach up and claw the bottom out of my little, wooden boat.

It had happened before.

*   *   *

It was August 29, 1911. The fog had lifted a bit when the yacht *Gunilda* exited Superior and steamed into the reef-lined Schreiber Channel.

With her sleek lines, huge bowsprit and tall masts, the palatial *Gunilda* had the racy lines of a sailing yacht. Built in Scotland in 1897, the 195-foot-long gold-plater had already cruised extensively throughout the world. Even in the great age of luxury steam yachts, she was considered one of the most elegant boats afloat.

The elderly Capt. Alexander Corkum, who had spent most of his life sailing on the Great Lakes, was at the helm. At his command was a crew of 20. The year before, he piloted the *Gunilda* to Duluth.

Her owner, William L. Harkness, thought he had little to worry about as he ordered his captain to sail up to Nipigon Bay. From his viewpoint, the channel was wide and clear.

This was magnificent country, the furthest point north on the lake. Forests of trees climbed up the mountains; round, green islands emerged boldly in little hills from the blue waters.

Aboard, Harkness' well-heeled guests enjoyed the amenities that a New York Yacht Club gold-plater could offer. White-coated stewards wheeled drinks around on trolleys; music tinkled from grand pianos — an elegant cruise in an age of opulence.

In his mahogany-lined chartroom, Capt. Corkum frowned uneasily. This was his first visit to Schreiber's reef-strewn waterway, and frankly he had doubts of how well the channel was charted.[1]

"Perhaps we should hire a local pilot," Capt. Corkum suggested.

"How much?" Harkness asked.

"About $25."

"Outrageous!" thundered the owner. "No."

It was difficult to believe that Harkness was a wealthy partner in the Standard Oil Co.

*   *   *

The *Gunilda's* sleek bow cut through blue waters, favoring the Copper Island side of the channel, away from upcoming Cat Island and its string of reefs to the southeast.

Her 20-foot-long bowsprit pointed the way northwest with a sweeping gesture; below decks, her triple-expansion steam engines pulsed. The run looked clear.

Suddenly, with a great groan followed by grinding noises of steel, about 80 feet of the *Gunilda* rose into the air, her bowsprit pointing upward. The hull lurched to starboard, then came to a heart-sickening stop.

Capt. Corkum peered into the clear waters. Just below the surface laid a dark gray mass, its peak disappearing into the chill depths. They had run their 600-ton yacht aground on McGarvey Shoal, the pinnacle of a huge, underwater mountain covered by only a few feet of water — unseen by the helmsman.[2]

Heavily grounded on the shoal, the *Gunilda's* bow rose a full five feet above the water and her stern sagged low in the water. Frantically, the crew made an emergency inspection, but she was not taking on any water, thanks to her rugged, all-steel construction. Her heavy sailboat keel had taken the brunt.

In a motor lifeboat, Harkness roared to the shore, about six miles away, where he clumped up the hill to the Rossport Inn. He set a telegram to his insurance company, telling them of his boat's grounding and demanding help to get his yacht off the rocks.

A day later from Port Arthur, the tug *James Whalen*, the most powerful tug on the lake, steamed around Copper Island and pulled alongside the yacht. The passengers and most of the crew were taken off the grounded vessel.

At the Rossport Inn, rounds of cheer were poured, and the

passengers' spirits lifted. They had just come through a minor scrape, but no one was hurt. It was an adventure — something to talk about back in New York.

Out on the shoal, the tugboat captain worried the *Gunilda* might founder when she was pulled off. Captain Scagel wanted to send for another barge and link it to the barge they'd towed here. The two would provide buoyancy and stability to the *Gunilda's* stern as she slid off the reef. Or so he reasoned.

"No!" stormed the penny-pinching millionaire, feeling that the locals were out to fleece him. It was his final mistake.

*   *   *

The tug ran twelve-inch manila hawsers to the *Gunilda,* and with a plume of smoke, began her tow. At first the big ship held steady on the reef. A second attempt, with more power, and she shuddered, beginning to move off the reef.

Skidding backwards, rocking on her keel, the *Gunilda* took on a hard list to starboard. Too late, Capt. Corkum saw open ports and hatchways. As they dipped under, she began to fill with water.

"Cut the lines," the tug captain roared. Crewmen grabbed for fire axes and frantically chopped at the groaning hawsers. Superior poured in the *Gunilda's* open portholes.

They barely saved the *Whalen* as the *Gunilda* went down, slipping backward off the pinnacle, bubbles of air pouring from her sinking hull. The sinking took about 20 minutes.

Stern first, she sank to the bottom of the shoal in 265 feet of water. There she came to rest, grand pianos, beautifully carved woodwork, and all — a millionaire's practically new yacht sitting upright without a hole in her.

The tug captain had been right. Two barges on either side would have provided her with enough reserve buoyancy to float off without harm. She certainly would not have taken the fatal list to one side. He also had been correct in positioning his crew with axes to cut the lines as she went under. Otherwise, the tug also would have been carried below.

A shaken Harkness sent a telegram to his insurance company, telling it of the loss. The company representatives reminded him he had insured her for only $100,000, a fraction of her worth. Once again, his attempt to pinch pennies had cost him dearly.

Undeterred, Harkness threw a party at the Rossport Inn. When the innkeeper asked him if he was grieving over his beautiful sunken ship, he replied with a measure of bravura: "Don't worry. They're still making yachts."

But when he returned to New York, the tragedy had caught up with him. Harkness appeared as if he had lost a daughter.

*   *   *

Below me, in her cold watery grave, the *Gunilda* is well preserved, just sitting on the bottom, and for all appearances, ready to sail away.

"It is difficult to imagine what a private yacht built in those days must look like," Ned Basher had told me. "There aren't many yachts left from that era, and this one's in mint condition. It was only a few years old when it sank, and it doesn't have a hole in it."

Called the most beautiful sunken ship in the world, she inevitably attracted dreams of glory to bring her back up, like a Lake Superior *Titanic*. Legends grew about a safe onboard containing millions of dollars in jewels.

In the 1930's, hard hat divers looked for ways to salvage the luxury yacht, but without success. In 1967 and 1968, one salvager attempted to bring up the *Gunilda* with grappling hooks. The attempt only pulled the *Gunilda* 50 feet deeper on the underwater pinnacle, sliding her from 265 feet to about 290 feet. The grappling hooks tore up parts of the otherwise intact sunken vessel.[3]

Marine salvager, Fred Broennle, of Thunder Bay, with his partner Charles King Hague, became interested in the wreck. One August day in 1970, Hague donned diving gear, and against all diving rules, went down alone. The plan was to go 80 feet under the water in an exploratory dive, but Hague decided to go deeper. He was lost, a suspected victim of nitrogen narcosis — rapture of the deeps. His body was not found.

Years later, a remote-controlled television camera was sent

down on the *Gunilda*, the first look in 70 years of the magnificent yacht. From the control room in a ship above the reef, Broennle watched as the camera photographed the area beside the sunken yacht.

Suddenly, a foot with a diver's flipper came into view; then the picture of a man on his back, two SCUBA tanks strapped to his back. To his horror, Broennle had found his long lost partner — still down at the bottom of Superior — a body preserved almost perfectly. Work with a grappling hook brought the lost diver to the surface.[4]

The wreck has claimed more divers. In 1989, Reg Barett of Brampton Ontario, was lost as he attempted this deep dive. Several more divers have been injured.

*   *   *

Ned Basher has long had an interest in the *Gunilda*. When I was at his Rossport Inn, he showed me a model of the *Gunilda* he had built. As I peered beneath the glass case, I could see the sleek yacht's beautiful shape. Outside, a Canadian flag flapped from atop one of the *Gunilda's* masts.[5]

Basher notes that the shipwreck has come full circle, "from beautiful wreck[6] to cultural heritage." SCUBA diving has evolved, he said, and "what was once a dive out of the limits of most divers now is possible for many.[7] Because the boat is in such pristine condition and has so many artifacts, it will be difficult to prevent looting."

He surprised me. "Maybe the answer is to have an authorized group go down and take off what is salvageable and have a public museum in Rossport. The boat will still be down there for divers, but face it, only a small part of the population will ever dive.[8] This way, many people can enjoy artifacts from the boat."

*   *   *

In the channel, I paused for a moment, drifting lightly. I bowed my head in reverence to the memory of the "Reluctant Lady of McGarvey Shoal," somewhere down there in her deep grave, far beneath my bobbing hull.

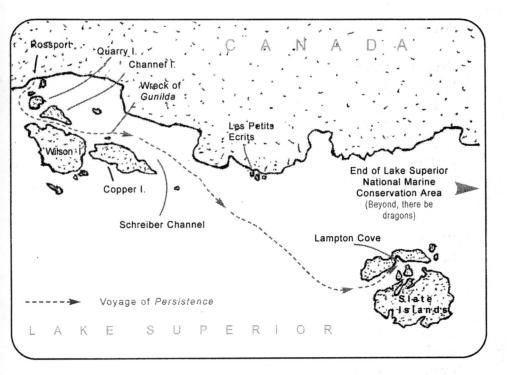

Chapter Twenty Four

RENDEZVOUS
IN THE
SLATES

All that we see or seem
is but a dream within a dream
— Edgar Allen Poe

O FF IN THE DISTANCE, the Slate Islands rose up to greet me. With blue peaks emerging out of a light hazing of mist, they looked to me like strange little Pacific atolls.

I was leaving the archipelago of islands and entering the open waters. To the east was one of the most remote areas of the lake with few harbors and marinas. It was a rugged, wind-swept shoreline — the North Shore's most unprotected part.

Beyond the protection of the friendly islands, *Persistence* picked up the motion of the light waves and began her dance with wind and water. I was enjoying the day's bright sunlit morning and blue skies, blending to the west with gentle, white, fluffy clouds.

I was now at the height of the arc of the lake, the northern-most part. I had been traveling mostly northeast from Grand Portage; now I was traveling southeast.

I was, once again, alone on the waters.

The boat was handling the swells in good order, and I was well pleased with her. Before I left, I had tightened up the line holding down my damaged rudder, checked the bilges for rising water, stocked up on drinking water and checked my food supply.

I also had trimmed my beard. We were now prepared for anything.

We were moving smartly, gaining speed. My GPS was showing 5.9, 6.1 and 6.3 m.p.h., a good speed for a 20-foot sailboat. I moved into my inside steering position, my remote control in my hand.

The autopilot would keep us on course across the open waters to the Slates. I'd sit back and relax in my inside wooden seat, my feet on both sides of the centerboard trunk — hoping I wouldn't get splashed today.

I snapped between GPS screens, which showed my heading, my speed, and the distance to my first landmark, as well as my ETA (estimated time of arrival). From the rocks at the mouth of the channel to the entry of the Slates was about 15 miles.

We'd do it easy in 2 hours 46 minutes, my GPS said, though I noted we had slowed a bit as the bow bit into a small wave. The GPS hurriedly made the minute correction.

Time to enjoy a little of the spectacular scenery. I looked out my plastic window and, appearing to the north were Les Petits Ecrits,[1] a group of distinctive high islands rising off the rugged shoreline.

The canoe brigades of the voyageurs of old visited here, a traditional rest area on the way up or down the Big Lake. I could make out a narrow channel between the islands.

My boat sailed on southeastward under hot sunshine and blue skies. I was heading for a channel between the Slate Islands, between Barnard Point and William Point.

And I also was heading for a rendezvous with a memory.

* * *

The Slate Islands peaks grew steadily. What looked like one solid peaked mountain, something out of the South Pacific, widened out into two distinct islands. As I entered the channel, my bow guided between steep bluffs on either side.

My GPS landmark was right on the money. I was off the lake, in calm water, and now looking for my home for the night in Lampton Cove.

I scooted warily up the channel, mindful of a string of reefs off William Point. Tall, heavily wooded cliffs came steeply down to the water's edge, close by my boat. I moved to the open cockpit, basking in the sunshine, and glanced below. The waters were clear[2], and I could see the bottom moving beneath me.

What a marvel the Slate Islands were today. High rounds of wooded islands stuck almost straight out of clear waters. I began to hum a snatch of a song from the musical *South Pacific*, something about "my own special island."

On my chart, the Slates were actually eight islands in all: two large islands, Patterson Island to the South, and Mortimore Island to the North, with several small islands in the middle and a couple more off to the east. I was in the center channel.

What had given them this unusual shape? The islands, experts theorized, were formed a billion years ago by an asteroid's impact. Just looking around me, I could believe the incredible, vast forces that had been at work.

I was now trying to locate Kate Rock. Kate was a well-defined reef, marked with an x on my Canadian chart. But I had been warned that in the Slates, "things can get a little confusing."

Off to starboard appeared a series of rocks. Kate Rock? I checked my GPS coordinates and thought, well, it could be.

There was only one way to be certain, but I wasn't about to try the depths with my keel near that reef.

I was interested in Kate Rock because that marked my entry to Lampton Cove. I circled around and came within a dozen yards of a steep-to island, but I could not identify the opening for certain.

With some surprise, I saw the landmark coordinates I had punched in my GPS were now reversing themselves. I had overshot Kate Rock and the cove.

I was in no hurry. I kept moving through the channel between the islands, enjoying the scenery. As I neared the end of the main island chain, between Mortimore and Patterson islands, I throttled back, engine burbling lightly, and paused, aware of the special moment.

This was it: the farthest east I would go.

Beyond the Slates stretched the broad, open waters of Superior. The island archipelago I had been in ended here at the Slates. And so did the boundary of the world's largest freshwater conservation area.[3]

Time to turn around to find my home for the night. I was moving back through the channel, searching for the elusive cove, when I heard the sound of another engine. I signaled to the small powerboat coming down the channel and he slowed as I pulled alongside. He looked surprised to see another boater.

"Where's Lampton Cove?" I shouted to make myself heard over the noise of the engines.

"Back there," he indicated with a wave of his arm, "is a channel. I don't know what it's called, but it's the only one around. It'll be a couple of miles back on your right."

He powered up his speedboat, and I watched him as he headed southward down a beautiful channel with overhanging trees, and disappeared behind a small island. He'd obviously been here a few times before.

Moving westward, I kept my eyes to starboard. Once again the magic of the shoreline opened up to me. From this direction, it looked like it might be the beginning of a cove, rather than just another in-and-out part of the island's waterline. I entered cautiously, watching my depth sounder.

I followed the curve of the island until ahead of me lay a large rocky outcropping running down to the water's edge. I moved cautiously around it. I emerged in waters about 10 to 12 feet deep, so clear it was like flying over air. You could see all the way down to the bottom rocks.

At the base of a rocky outcropping was a small, wooden dock. I had planned to anchor in the cove, but a dock was terrific — and, it turned out to be just big enough for my little sailboat.

I threw out my fenders and came alongside. I unclipped my safety harness, and docking lines in hand, stepped off and tied up in Lampton Cove.

I heard a fluttering of large wings, and up on the rocky shore, a huge, white seagull came to rest. He stared at me with his wide eyes, and I stared back at him. He was a special bird, not only large but blindingly white. He paced back and forth on the rocks about 25 feet from me, looking my way.

In the sunlight, this imperious old sea bird looked slightly spectral.

I had thought these islands were too far out, too primitive to support the birds that normally are everywhere inland. But here this old bird was, walking about, and keeping me company. How had he gotten here? Why was he here now?

The late afternoon sun bored hotly down on me, and I ignored the seagull to pull off my protective gear and get down to my T shirt and jeans. As I stepped off the dock and onto the rocks that led up to the timber line, I had the distinct impression I had stepped back into summer and another point in history.

I walked up the smooth rock formation, exploring my solitary domain. My friend the seagull had taken off. Maybe he'd return.

I thought of the story about the old sailor from Thompson Island who said that if he ever died and came back, it'd be as a seagull.

A thought crossed my mind. I'd come back to it later.

*   *   *

It was time to explore. About 50 feet down the rock, something caught my eye near the water's edge — a giant metal ring lying against the brown rocks. It was perhaps a foot across, forged out of iron, an inch thick, and heavily rusted. As I hefted it up a few inches in my hand, I saw it was massively fastened into the rock.

It was an old-fashioned mooring ring for a long-gone ship. I lifted my eyes. Across the cove, just up from the water's edge, was an outcropping of rock, surrounded by brush and trees. I cupped my hands to my eyes to get a little better focus. In the shadows was a cave, the entry to an old mining claim.

So that was why the mooring ring was here. Depending on weather and wind direction, the old ships would come into the cove and tie up here off this outcropping of rock, or over by the cave. I wondered if they found anything of value on these islands. Silver or gold.[4] I figured that if it had become famous, such as Silver Islet, I would have run across some history.

I walked back to the boat and stepped aboard, settling in. We were home for the night in the Slates. The seagull was nowhere in sight, and I was alone but happy.

Time slowed. As the day lowered into twilight and the evening colors painted the western sky, the deep pines blended into dark shadows. The water turned an incredible blue, catching just a little of the sky's red pallet.

I thought I saw a movement on the northern shore. A tall animal with a rack of antlers and huge hoofs was along the water's edge. A woodland caribou. He was moving slowly, lowering his head, browsing his evening meal.

As I watched, the caribou[5] sauntered off until he was lost in the darkness of the woods.

I was alone again. There was a stillness in this island that seemed to press its presence upon me. Darkness was coming to my little boat and myself.

I stared outside the portlight, my thoughts turning inward. They were filled with a sailor's memories, of other voyages on the lake. Bright days, cool nights, good companionship.

Inevitably my thoughts turned to Albert Leon.

* * *

In 1984, on my voyage from the Apostle Islands into Thunder Bay, I met the old Thunder Bay shipwright. With the majestic Sleeping Giant in the background, I had been tied up in beautiful Prince Arthur's Landing Marina, waiting for his boat to return from his wanders through the islands he loved so much.

One day, there she was, bobbing gently by a grassy embankment not far from me, her wooden masts jauntily reaching toward the heavens, her sails laced to her booms. It was the *Carioca,* the wooden boat of Thunder Bay shipwright and sailor Albert Leon.

He had a white beard and wore the dark clothing traditional to seafaring men. He was seated in the cockpit of his old ketch and was gazing absently into the distant horizon. He may have seen something I did not see, heard something I couldn't hear. He seemed to have a seafarer's hundred-league stare.

I started to introduce myself, but he already knew who I was.

"Do you want a beer?" he offered, and he told me that his boat was sinking. I stepped on board and settled down in the cockpit, beer in hand.

The late afternoon sun gave us a pleasant warmth. He had hit a reef, but he did not seem overly concerned. I looked below. Creeping water was visible over the floorboards.

"I thought I had run out of luck," he said. "I hit hard, but a couple of large waves came along and boosted the whole boat — bouncing me from one rock to another — and finally just shoved me off."

"Amazing good luck," I said, trying to imagine what had happened. His old, wooden boat had bounced sideways across the reefs in high winds and seas. The old shipwright had emerged shaken and with a badly leaking boat. Undaunted, he had sailed it back to harbor.

As we had another beer, he looked patiently downward into

the cabin. "The damage may swell up or realign itself," he said, hopefully.

I leaned back in the cockpit of the slowly sinking boat, feeling the sun on my shoulders and the gentle fall wind on my face. Albert was a legend in Thunder Bay, and if he had faith, I guess I should, too.

The old shipwright was again gazing off into space. My eyes followed. There was something distant in the mists of the horizon, beyond the harbor. It was shining, white —-maybe a sail. Then it was gone.

As I left, I asked if there was anything I could do.

"Take a bearing from time to time on my masts and the stars," he told me. "If my masts aren't up there, you know I am in trouble."

"Sure enough," I agreed, and walked back go my own boat. And from time to time, as the night passed, I got up and looked over at his old wooden boat. His masts were always true and bold against the harbor lights, pointing up at the heavens.

After my voyage was done, I returned to my home in Shoreview, but I kept in touch with the old shipwright. He worked as the master builder[6] at Fort William. From time to time, I had driven up to visit him aboard the historic schooner he was building for the old fur fort.

It was on this voyage in CPR Slip, when Lynda Blanchette, aboard the *Ogima*, broke the news to me. He had died.

"We were his friends," she said. "And we carried out his request to take his ashes out to his favorite place"

"And that is..?"

"The Slates."

And here I was. It grew dark around my boat in this solitary harbor. Waves gently lapped against my wooden hull. But I felt at ease and in a sort of comfort, for I felt I was not alone.

Somewhere here the old shipwright's ashes rested — and, possibly, his restless spirit.

A fellow sailor would understand.

On the beach: The once-mighty *Yennek*

Chapter Twenty Five

GRAND OLD MAN
OF THE
INLAND SEAS

What we have once loved we can never lose,
all that we love deeply becomes a part of us.
— Helen Keller

DAWN CAME EARLY. I saw the first rosy blushes over the treetops, painting the little harbor. I rolled out of my bunk, greatly refreshed, and made myself a latte. Steaming mug in hand, I surveyed my little harbor. I could relax and find a home here.

But it wasn't in the cards. It was time to return.

I snapped on the VHF, which told me I'd have fair skies, sunshine, and a light wind. Waves would also be light.

I frowned. This did not feel right to me. I had begun my

Superior voyage in a storm. Ending it with such nice weather seemed anticlimactic — a letdown.

It was easy to get away from the dock. All I did was grab the little boat, give it a shove backward, and hop on board. *Persistence* moved in these calm waters like a canoe, stirring up just a few ripples.

I moved easily down the channel between the islands and entered the open waters. Here it was just as billed: bright skies, waves less than a meter in height, and light winds out of the southwest.

The Schreiber Channel seemed wide and clear, the islands tall and friendly.

My return sail was beautiful. A day out of Disneyland, but as I neared Rossport, I saw that all the dock spaces were filled. A minor problem, but where was I going to put my boat?

Circling slowly alongside the dock, I saw the dock boy come out of his shack. "Where can I tie up?" I hollered across the water.

"Next door," he yelled back. "Lady says it's OK."

Odd, I thought. Someone was going to loan me the use of their own personal dock? Just like that? It seemed too generous and hospitable to be true, but I swung my bow to the east.

Past the government dock and the trimaran that blocked my view, I saw a private dock extending out into the water. As I headed toward it, a woman looked up and began walking out to meet me.

I waved and she waved back. Friendly. Hospitable. It would be all right, I decided.

"Wham." I heard the unmistakable sound of my centerboard banging against the bottom, and I felt the familiar vibration in the hull. About 30 feet from the dock, we came to a halt.

We had done it again. Run aground on a rock.

But we were old hands at this by now. "Just a moment," I said, ducking below and yanking on the centerboard pennant. With the centerboard up, we scooted over the rocks and alongside the dock.

"Thanks, " I said. "I appreciate it."

"You're welcome," she said, taking my dock lines and helping me tie up. "We have the space, and you are welcome to use it."

My benefactor was Colleen Kenney and I was at the waterfront home of Ray Kenney, age 91, a grand old man of the lake. Ray was in his wheelchair when I went into the house. At the water's edge, I had passed a battered old boat up on blocks, her dented hull covered with rusty patches, her wooden cabin showing rot. She was the *Yennek*, Ray's old boat.

Captain Kenney is an ex-school principal. He taught in Canadian schools for 40 years during the winters and "boated summers," taking out charter parties in his all-metal powerboat. The *Yennek*, I learned, is his name spelled backwards.

"Some say throw it in the garbage," Ray said sadly. "But it is almost a historic boat."

I listened intently, for I love old boats.

The old man in the wheelchair spun a tale of his boat and their many adventures together. The *Yennek* took historians, scientists, adventurers, journalists, and cameramen out on the watery route to the islands. It helped the Cousteau series explore Lake Superior. *National Geographic* magazine chartered her for a feature article and photography on the Slates. She was in television programs and movies. In the course of her duties, she saw many high seas.

"A cameraman wanted to get a scene out in the rough seas," Ray recalled with a small smile. "So we took the *Yennek* out into some big waves. In the troughs we were so far down we were out of sight."

"Get the pictures?"

Ray shook his head. "We had to do it all over again. The cameraman had run out of film."

"And?"

"When we saw it later, the film just showed the flag above the waves. He never got any pictures of the heavy stuff." He laughed. The cameraman had frozen up behind his lens.

He has met Superior's famed "Three Sisters,"[1] a combination of three waves, each larger than the first. "You get on top of the Three Sisters on a boat like the *Yenneck*, you get quite a ride. But be careful or you can bury yourself."

He added, "If you make a mistake out there on Superior you usually pay for it."

Ray's *Yennek*, a 28-footer, was built in 1947 with an all-steel bottom, "thick and tough," Ray said. "Armor plate." She was originally powered by a big inboard Lycoming engine, which was replaced by a Chrysler T120 in 1948.

"You get storms with 45-foot waves off Battle Island," he recalled. On the island were diesel tanks anchored with steel straps 42 feet above the water level. "We had a storm come in and toss them in the bush."

He added, "A 500-gallon tank anchored at the base of the lighthouse disappeared. They never found it again."

He also has vivid memories of the *Edmund Fitzgerald*. The "*Big Fitz*," he said, "we saw from about a half mile away or so. Boy, was she a rusty looking old hulk." He recalls saying to his wife, "Does she ever look in tough shape."

He also saw her before she disappeared. He was "going to work" the day of the terrible storm, Nov. 10, 1975, and when he got out of the Schreiber Channel and into the open seas, he hit "tremendously big waves." The wind was out of the northeast — a dreaded northeaster.

Though late in the season, he had to get some campers off an island. On the return trip, waves worked their way over his boat's deck. Even the mighty *Yenneck* lumbered and pitched under their power. "The waves hit you, and hit you so hard, it was like someone taking a big, big sledge hammer and hitting you."

The campers were terrified. "Don't worry," one man told Ray, "we'll NEVER come back." Ray remembers they were true to their word. He never saw them again. That night, the *Fitzgerald*[2] went down.

"When you try to compete with nature, man's best works are pretty fragile," Ray said. And as for Superior: "Love it, respect it, particularly, its might."

*   *   *

I left him there, the grand old captain of Rossport, sitting with his memories, and walked down the grassy slope to the water's edge. Ahead of me lay the *Yennek*, drawn up out of the water.

With her plumb powerboat bow, the *Yennek* must have been a powerful looking brute punching through the waves. But four decades of service had taken a lot out of her.

I moved closer, moving my hand along her hull. Worn in her metal were memories of her lifetime, mute testimony of the mountains of water she shoved aside and the storms she braved.

Her silver painted hull was scratched and dented; patches of rust showed through. The entire hull near the waterline had a series of creases, bumps, and hollows, the result of decades of warfare with immoveable objects.

She was old and worn, but to my eyes she was still a noble vessel.

Yeah. I love old boats.

She deserved better than to be lying beside the water, rusting and rotting away.

*   *   *

It was warm today, with just a wisp of wind out of the west as I began walking.

My mind was on Ray's old boat.

A boat of a thousand memories. The last surviving vessel of an epic time in tiny Rossport's history.

Up a narrow road that winds up the hill, just south of the railroad tracks, I stopped and looked around. Here, in the middle of the tall grass, was a quiet meadow with a sweeping view of the beautiful Rossport harbor and the outlying islands.

An idea came to me.

I had found the perfect place

In my mind's eye, I could envision the repristinated *Yennek*, with her steel hull faired and painted, her cabin bright once more, her chromed spotlight focused ahead and sparkling in the sunlight.

She'd be here on a proper boat cradle, with her bow lifted

high to Superior, as if about to sail off into the misty horizon.

She'd be on display here — an old boat with a soul that lived again.

There'd be a small sign with a bird's eye view of the islands she'd visited so often.

Maybe a car with some tourists would drive by and some little kid would lean out the window and say, "What's that?" and his parents would read aloud about the boat of Rossport and the remarkable old skipper and the voyages the two had been through together.

A little lump came to my throat.

I would like that. A lot.

And so would Ray Kenney.

Photo / Dave Nixon

Hauled from its watery grave, the powerboat The *Beef* is a total loss after overturning in high seas during a storm off Stockton Island in the Apostle Islands.

Chapter Twenty Six

MORE STORM TALES: THE AWFUL GREEN SKY

All that which concerns the sea is profound and final.
The sea provides visions, darknesses, revelations.
— Hilaire Belloc

THROUGHOUT MY VOYAGE, I was hearing stories of boaters who also had encountered the Fourth of July Green Storm. So far, I had heard first-hand tales of individual survival, but my knowledge was incomplete. In the islands, I had been out of touch with news reports.

I'd learn more when I returned to my office.

The storm had been tricky. It seemed to have come out of nowhere, bounded across the Sawtooth Mountains and swept onto the lake, where it found me. That much I knew about the storm.

So far on this voyage, I'd encountered what appeared to be the main blast of the storm, with hail-like rain and extremely high winds. In the Fourth of July Green Storm, my boat got repeatedly knocked down, and, for a while seemed unable to come back up.

I'd been lucky. When I finally got into the shelter of an island, I found that the only damage to my boat was some lost fenders and a broken alarm clock.

I had a few new bruises on me.

But I was acquiring new information all the time as boaters got together and talked. I soon learned that the storm did not end on the northern shores of Lake Superior.

Across the lake, in the Apostle Islands area off the northern shores of Wisconsin, the storm also hit hard.

One boater was pushing hard to reach the safety of the Bayfield harbor and the city dock when he saw "an awful green sky" coming at him.

"When the rain hit," he later told me, "I couldn't see the end of my boat."

Ed Ferlauto, commodore of the Shorewood Yacht Club in Minnesota, was onboard his 31-foot Island Packet in Port Superior when the Fourth of July storm rolled in.

"There was lightning, the sky turned dark, and the howling started," Ed said. "There were gale-force winds. And it seemed like it never stopped."

The weather remained turbulent and unsettled for days.

"I never experienced a significant storm period for that long," he said. "There were so many storms, it was incredible."

*   *   *

In the Boundary Waters Canoe Area wilderness, up along the Canadian border to the north and west of me, a small seaplane hurriedly landed at a small lake.

"There's a big storm heading this way," the pilot yelled to a boater who was headed to the safety of his cabin. "And we can't outrun it."

The pilot and a companion taxied to shore and tied their seaplane to a sheltered part of the lake. They hopped aboard the top of the plane's wings.

When the storm hit, the winds tore the tops of trees, and the rain flew horizontally over the lake. The seaplane bobbed about wildly, with its passengers desperately hanging on to each end of the wings. The plane, and passengers, remarkably survived.

Later, the boater flew over the windstorm area. "You could actually see the path of the storm," he told me. "The trees in the valleys are still intact, but the tops of the hills are denuded. It must have been a tremendous straight-line wind."

I could personally attest to that.

*   *   *

There had been a number of remarkable tales of survival during the storm and in the turbulent days that followed in its wake.

But now I heard of the first boat that went down. The surprise to me is that I never expected it to happen to this person.

At age 66, Dave Nixon is one of the most experienced boaters on Superior — and has rescued more than 400 boats. A wise, senior counselor of the lake and its ways, Dave is charter master of Superior Charters, located in the Apostle Islands — one of the biggest sailing organizations in the U.S. berthed in a single harbor.

I've admired Dave's boat, The *Beef*, a brute of a power craft that he keeps tied near his office. The 23-foot Seacraft is powered by two 140-h.p. OMC outboards, and Dave swears by the way the hull handles heavy weather.

"Best heavy weather hull for its size ever made," he told me.

Over the years, The *Beef* has survived a lot of rough weather on Superior. Except this season.

Several days after the Fourth of July storm, Dave got a distress call from one of his charter vessels. The *Aquila*. The 32-foot Islander sloop had been riding easy at anchor when the seas started building from the northeast.

Photo / Dave Nixon
Dave Nixon watches as a crane deposits The *Beef* on a Stockton Island beach.

The day had been pleasant in Julian Bay, off the Presque Isle Point on the east shore of Stockton Island.

But trouble began when the crew started the sailboat's engine and tried to free up its anchor. The *Aquila* overrode the anchor line and caught it in the prop. It wrapped tightly, killing the engine.

Powerless, the boat went stern-to the building seas. Waves began to splash over the transom.

The *Beef* roared out of Port Superior to the rescue, but Dave and charter captain Kevin Buzicky quickly found that the North Channel was alive with big rollers.

To get some protection, Dave gunned his powerboat into the lee of Madeline Island, and then made a dash across the channel to Stockton. He followed the protected south side of the island around to Presque Isle Point.

A slash of green water over the bow greeted The *Beef* as she encountered the open waters. With seas to eight feet in height and building, Dave throttled back to get his powerboat off plane. He began to quarter the waves to make progress.

The Coast Guard had been contacted, but it was not responding immediately to the sailboat's call. Dave saw that a

National Park Service vessel was circling the disabled *Aquila*.

The sailboat was in trouble, held stern-to the oncoming surf, with waves boarding the cockpit. The anchorage was open to the seas and unprotected. The waves were building.

Dave worked his way to the side of the disabled sailboat, and Captain Buzicky jumped aboard the *Aquila*. Dave circled slowly, trying to get a line on the sailboat when a large wave invaded The *Beef's* stern.

Water shot over the side, dousing and killing both engines.

He threw out an anchor, and after The *Beef* came bow to the waves, Dave attempted to get his engines fired up again. One failed to start; the other outboard began idling slowly, but would not put out any power.

Automatic bilge pumps began to whir and discharge green water.

"The seas continued to board over the bow of the boat," Dave told me. "And we were slowly filling up."

Fighting his way to the bouncing bow, Dave strained to pull up the anchor. He found that the line was under so much tension he had to cut the rode with his knife.

" I thought the surf would drift us into the sand beach," he said.

Without its anchor, The *Beef* began drifting. Dave attempted to steer, but without power, the boat turned beam to the oncoming growlers. About 150 yards from shore, the powerboat was struck by a big wave.

"It happened fast," Dave said. "As it went over, I grabbed the T-top and scooted out."

The boat flipped over and sank.

"The water was cold," he said. But he had on his Mustang floatation jacket and swam to shore through the surf, where he pulled himself up on the beach.

The National Park Service boat attempted to turn the *Aquila* around to face the waves. But the rescue attempt failed as the sailboat's fouled anchor let go.

Dave watched as the sailboat floated into shore, then canted to one side on its keel. The crew jumped off and waded ashore; Dave joined them for a hike to the Presque Isle Bay Dock.

Later that evening, the Coast Guard arrived at the island and took them back to their station in Bayfield, Wisconsin. It had been remarkable that no one had been injured.

Days later, Dave took out the tug *Eclipse*, under the command of Ron Nelson, to pull the sailboat off the beach. Even after lying on its side in heavy surf, the disabled boat was in remarkably good shape.

It had several cracked ribs and a bent rudder. But the engine and prop were still OK. A little work and she'd go back into service.

But not so with The *Beef*.

It was a sad day when Dave took the *Eclipse* to locate his beloved powerboat. A diver went below to secure her in straps and haul her from her watery grave.

Dave had recovered his beloved boat, but her life as a rescue boat was done.[1]

Chapter Twenty Seven

MEL GIBSON'S
MYSTERY BOAT

*Not everything that can be counted counts,
and not everything that counts can be counted.*
—Albert Einstein

L ATE IN THE AFTERNOON, as the sun cast surreal long shadows over the waterfront, I noticed a number of boaters gathering on the south side of the dock. They were pointing excitedly at something entering the Rossport harbor.

Shading my eyes with my hand, I looked to the southwest. Even from a distance, she looked huge with her many levels of decks towering up from the waterline. She had a mean rake to her.

As she maneuvered out of Nipigon Bay and past Whiskey Island,[1] heading for the channel between Quarry and Healey islands, she presented her stern. She had two huge hulls. A giant catamaran, the likes of which I'd never seen, was more than a hundred feet in length.

A dock boy drifted by, a knowing look on his face.

"What?" I said.

"Mel Gibson's boat," he announced proudly. He caught my look. "It's confirmed. He's onboard. He arrived by helicopter in Thunder Bay."

The giant catamaran slowed, and a white inflatable shoved off and roared toward us, loaded to the gunnels. Throttling back when it reached the inside of the dock, it headed for the boat-loading ramp.

Two white-uniformed crewmen tied up, stepped off, and deposited several dozen large, plastic bags near the dockside trash container.

One crew member sauntered off. A few of the crowd gathered around.

"Mel's boat?" Someone had to ask.

The Australian sailor aboard the inflatable looked up good humouredly. "No," he said. "But we've been having a lot of fun with that rumor since it started."

Definitely not Mel, he assured us. "Nobody of that name aboard."

The crowd around me lost interest, and the Australian, in his crisp white crew uniform and white shoes, sat biding his time in the all-white inflatable.

After a while, the other crew member returned from his errand and clambered on board. They left in a flurry of high-speed spray.

The catamaran had sailed up the channel between Quarry and Healey islands and was lost to sight. The inflatable followed their wake.

"Disappointment." I shrugged my shoulders, exchanging amused glances with one of the more animated dockside spectators, who was obviously having a lot of fun with the idea. "But who'd thought he'd show up here?"

Indeed, who would imagine that Mel Gibson, multimillionaire Australian film actor, Hollywood director, and Oscar win-

ner, would show up in this tiny hamlet in this remote part of
Superior? It boggled my imagination.

"Maybe not," the young sailor answered, with an edge to
her voice. She was off one of the large cruising sailboats that
had just arrived at the dock, and apparently, she was not going
to let go of her star-struck dream. "He does have a house[2] along
the North Shore, a spectacular, big one atop a hill."

"Eh?" I said.

"Three things," she said, ticking them off. "One, the crew
guy said only four people were on board, and I saw more than
that with my binoculars, including several children. Gibson
has a number of children."[3]

"Second?"

"The newspaper account was very specific about the helicopter flight into Thunder Bay. A cop took someone out to
look at the boat, which he identified as Gibson's."

I was intrigued. "And third?"

"That runabout looked like it might be taking somebody
aboard to come ashore, but they got put off by the crowd. A
movie star would act like that."

"You're good," I said. "Really good."

She smiled, pleased with herself, and I began to edge away.

"He's coming in, you know," she said, leaning forward con-
spiratorially, "under cover of dark."

I stopped and frowned. "What for?"

Excitement crept into her voice. " To eat at the inn."

"The big ship will come back?"

"Naw," she said. "A runabout. With Mel disguised as a crew
member."

I could not tell if she was pulling my leg or not. But I had
the feeling that she had read maybe one too many mystery nov-
els.

As I turned to go back to my boat, a thought crossed my
mind.

"You're going to keep the Mel watch?"

"Until dark," she said, a merry, conspiratorial glitter in her
eyes.

*   *   *

It was all very heady. Irresistible good fun. Here we were, a bunch of small-time boaters in this remote, little Canadian hamlet, sharing space with moose, bears, and endless water, but talking on a first-name basis about a Hollywood star.

It was not Mel Gibson anymore. But "Mel."

The next day, I checked on the young woman's Mel Watch.

"Had drinks with him last night," she announced proudly.

"He made it in?"

"Oh, sure," she said. "Partied all night."

"And?"

"Oh, he went back to his boat," she said with an exaggerated sigh.

"To think that I missed all the excitement," I said, giving her an exaggerated lofting of my eyebrows, Jim Carey style.

"And missed the story of the decade," she added. "Some writer."

For good measure, and to impress her of my sincerity, I threw in a deep sigh. She was not impressed.

*   *   *

All humorous dockside chit-chat aside, it was time to figure out what was actually going on. I remembered that when the first officer of the catamaran had disappeared from the docks, he had headed in the direction of the inn.

Slowly, I trudged up the hill to see Ned Basher at the Rossport Inn. Ned would know — he always seemed to be in the thick of things in Rossport. Ned was not only inn-keeper, but seemed to be Rossport's official greeter, unofficial hamlet manager, and all-around northwood's bon vivant.

Sure enough, I learned, the mysterious ship's officer had come up to see Ned and had a few beers with him.

Ned had the answers. The boat was named the *Moecca*, a 150-foot long, jet-drive catamaran, a state-of-the-art luxury boat that was registered in the Isle of Mann, under British registry. It had been built in Australia, but it flew the British, not the Australian, flag.

"The Mel Gibson rumor started with us at the Saint

Lawrence," the first officer had told Ned, "and stayed with us all the way up here."

With her international crew of British, Greeks, Italians, and Australians, the *Moecca* was kept constantly cruising to entertain corporate executives and important customers. She's a luxury yacht — a modern-day *Gunilda* — that's already sailed three-quarters of the way around the world.

You could charter her when she was not otherwise scheduled, I learned. A week on the *Moecca* went for $140,000, not including food, water, or beverages.

I brought Ned up to date on what I had heard on the docks. One of the rumors was that the big cat was coming in for parts.

Ned liked that one. "I've got lots of parts in the basement," he said with a grin. "If they don't fit, for Mel Gibson's boat, we'll make them fit." A little northwoods humor there.

"So what did they come in for?" I asked.

"GPS'."

I was surprised. "Don't they have GPS'[4] on that luxury barge?"

"Oh, the boat has all sorts of electronics," Ned said. "But two guests on board did not have their own personal GPS' and they were feeling kind of lost. They wanted their own."

Ah! The truth was out at last. The *Moecca* had been in radio contact with the Rossport Inn, and Basher had ordered the personal GPS' for the guests. The *Moecca* had dispatched the first officer and a crewman in a runabout to pick up the two hand-held units.

And to drop off the trash.

After a few beers, I trudged back down to my little boat and shook my head. Imagine, detouring a giant catamaran just to cater to the whims of two guests.

I remembered F. Scott Fitzgerald who said something like: The rich, they are very different from you and me.

*   *   *

Not so pleased with the arrival of "Mel's boat" was the lady at the Halcyon Haven, the harbor-side establishment that serviced boaters and fishermen.

"They came in with a runabout full of bags of garbage, and they piled them up in front of the garbage bin," she said, angrily. "And the haulers charge us $2 for every five bags."

"They didn't pay?"

She shook her head. "No. They sailed off in that big boat, and we're stuck with the bill."

She added that she did get a telephone call from a Duluth newspaper reporter who had been following the progress of Mel's boat.

"And I told them," she said, a gleam in her eye.

"About Mel? Or the boat?"

"No," she said. "About the garbage they left. The reporter asked me if I had opened any of it up and gone through it."

"Imagine going through garbage!" She was indignant. "Or suggesting it. I told them — no!"

Her eyes took on a gleam. "But I did tell them that we have to pay for picking up their garbage. Did you know the haulers charge us $2 for every five bags?"

At the Rossport dock, *Persistence* waits in the fog.

Chapter Twenty Eight

LAST DAYS
AT DOCKSIDE

Life is a succession of lessons,
which must be lived to be understood.
— Ralph Waldo Emerson

THE FOG HAD ROLLED IN and filled beautiful Rossport Harbor with a gush of white. Off in the distance, the island archipelago that guarded this little hamlet from the inland sea had disappeared in the fluid air.

In the mists, I could see the circle of boats at the dock, but nothing beyond. It was quiet, too. The fog was like a giant blotter, soaking up the noise. Nothing moved, no people, no vessels.

The end was coming for me, rolling in with the morning's

fog and with a pang of regret. Last night, I used a pay telephone located outside the dock master's shack to call home. It
would be good, so good, to see Loris and Will again.

It was time to go. I had accomplished my sail through the
island archipelago, but at a price. I was gobbling painkillers
regularly now, and they were not totally effective. The pain in
my left knee and ankle made my gait and my stance increas-
ingly wobbly. I was feeling all of my 66 years.

In preparation for hauling *Persistence* out of the water, I
already had begun to take down the little boat, unhanding the
sails and unsnapping the dodger.

I reached my fingers down into the bilge and felt the cold
and wet — about an inch of water in the bilge. The leak was
getting worse.

I snapped on my weather radio. "Strong thunderstorm warning," the Canadian weatherman announced, "with high winds."

I wasn't going out, but it looked like two sailboats were. I
hurried down the dock to talk to Joe Floyd and Rick
Munsinger.

"Getting underway?" I asked.

"Going to the Slates," Joe said. Rick, holding a coffee cup,
sauntered over.

"Heard the weather?" Both shook their heads, so I relayed
the storm warning.

"We'll keep an eye out," Joe said, nonchalantly. "Thanks for
the weather warning."

I shrugged my shoulders. "Have a good trip," I said.[1]

*   *   *

On Captain Kenney's private dock, I saw Harold and Joyce
Dahlgren, of West Point, Iowa, getting ready to go out in their
17-foot runabout.

Concerned, I walked over to see if they'd heard the storm
warning.

"We're not going far," Joyce said. "Just into the islands.
Ray is coming with us."

"He still goes out?" I tried not to let my surprise show.

"He used to take us out. Now we take him."

"We came into Canada about 27 years ago," Joyce explained. "And Harold and I stopped at Rossport. We met Ray, and we fell in love with the area. We've been back every summer. We used to go out with Ray in his Yennek until it got too old to go. Now we trailer our boat up and take him out. He's still showing us some of his favorite spots."

"Where are you going today?"

"Wherever Ray wants to go," she said.

I stopped and stared. "Look there," I said, alarmed.

It was Ray, down on his hands and knees, crawling slowly down the dock. "Does he need help?" I asked.

"Naw," Harold drawled. "He prefers to do it himself."

Captain Kenney had brought his wheelchair down to the water's edge and was making the rest of the way on his own down the dock.

"Need help?" Harold asked.

Ray shook his head. No. He was doing OK on his own.

"He really prefers to do it himself," the Iowa boater repeated, mostly for my benefit.

I got the message and felt a surge of pride. At age 91, this grand old mariner was once more going out into his beloved islands.

When Ray was aboard, the tall Iowan fired up his boat's outboards and the little fishing boat cut a wake through the blue harbor, bathed in sparkling morning sunlight. Off toward Quarry Island, a little fog was whisping about.

But that was not all that was coming in.

* * *

A heaviness hung in the air and clouds began to gather. A storm was rising. On the dock, my friend in the big trimaran was getting restless.

"I'm heading south," he announced.

"Where are you going?" I asked.

"Oh, I'll move from place to place, working as I need money. You know if you anchor off and stay away from commercial places, you really don't need much money."

I nodded. He was single, he was young, and he had a plan.

What's more, I had the feeling that he could live on almost nothing. At one point in time, so could I.

"Any idea where you'll end up?"

"Eventually I'll make my way down to Florida," he said. "And then I'll really be down south." He smiled happily at the thought.

*   *   *

Angry clouds swept in over the little harbor. Thunder rumbled and the day grew dark. I saw lightning flashes over the islands.

I ran to my sailboat and ducked below before the rain came sheeting down.

I thought of the old captain with the Iowa couple out in their little fishing boat.

Rain turned to hailstones. I could hear them thump and pound on my cabin roof. I was secure and dry — but what about them?

*   *   *

The storm rushed off and the sky grew bright. Evening started to fall, but I still saw no sign of the old mariner.

Then, in the lengthening rays of the sun, came the high-powered whine of outboards as they cut a shining wake in the harbor.

I hurried over to their dock. "Any trouble with the squall?" I inquired.

"Oh," the Iowa man said, "we saw the storm coming, so we just ducked into a little cove and waited it out. No problem. Then we went back to fishing."

"Catch anything?"

"Only a couple little ones."

But I caught it: the fisherman's nonchalance that belied the facts. Obviously, they had been to one of Ray's secret fishing spots and had done well. I glanced in the boat and looked at Ray.

Beneath the brim of his long-billed fishing cap, the old man's eyes twinkled proudly.[2]

Photo / Clive Dudley
The storm-swept sky sweeps out across Thunder Bay toward the Sleeping Giant.

Chapter Twenty Nine

SUPERIOR'S FAREWELL

The time comes when you realize that you haven't only been specializing in something — something has been specializing in you.
— Arthur Miller

WITH *PERSISTENCE* SECURED IN HER TRAILER, Loris and I drove down the winding Queen's Highway on our way home. We stopped in beautiful Thunder Bay for the night.

As evening came, we began walking to find someplace to celebrate my return from Superior. The restaurant that appealed to us had a lot of windows, skylights, and a large, outdoor patio. Tonight we'd dine alfresco.

We were seated at a table under a big umbrella on the restaurant's deck. To the northwest rose the rugged Canadian bluffs; below us spread the blue waters of the immense harbor. I noticed that the late afternoon had grown overly humid. The weight of the day was growing. It felt as if it were pressing down on me. "What's the matter?" Loris asked.

I nodded my head toward the building weather. The sky had turned gunmetal gray. Ominous, dark clouds were spilling over the Sawtooth range. "I'm glad I'm not out on Superior," I said. I was only partially joking.

"So am I," she said. She was grimly serious.

The pasta course arrived, and we dug in, but I kept glancing at the darkening sky. The clouds were rearing high – powerful-looking brutes. I saw their bases were starting to tear off and swirl, as if they had small tornadoes underneath.

"Time to move," I said. "I'm not finished," Loris said.

"Now!" I emphasized. We grabbed our plates and dashed inside. The manager slammed the glass doors behind us.

With a shriek, a great gust of wind slammed into where we had been seated. Umbrellas overturned, patio tables fell over, and chairs blew down. Things flew and crashed against the glass doors, threatening to burst inside.A waitress began to open the door. A manager yelled, "Don't go out there." Something hard hit the glass door.

I walked under the skylights and looked up at the sky. Through the glass I could see that dark clouds were rushing madly toward us, swirling trails of gray matter.

Fascinated, I motioned to the waitress. "Large cognac, please."

The heavens filled with the fireworks of the heavy weather, rushing past the puny mortals below. Minutes later, the waitress returned. "The bartender gave you the four star," she said, a little puzzled. "That'll do nicely. Thanks," I said.

Still looking upward, I raised my glass in salute. The windstorm turned into a rainstorm, dumping sheets upon the skylights. Thunder growled; lightning crackled. The wind howled, moving the storm onward. Spectacular.

But there was something else happening. Something I sensed in some odd way, but couldn't begin to explain. Something I felt in my heart.

In the midst of the rain, the howling winds, the billowing storm clouds, I knew. I truly knew. It came to me with the force of a revelation.

My old adversary. My love. It was Superior — giving me a proper send off. At last, Superior was saying farewell.

I took a big sip of my cognac.

Farewell, to you, too, my deadly love.

Part Three

EPILOGUE TO A VOYAGE

*Do not go where the path may lead;
go instead where there is no path
and leave a trail.
—Ralph Waldo Emerson*

Photo / Clive Dudley

Off Thompson Island, whitecaps on Superior crash relentlessly against the rugged shoreline.

Chapter Thirty

IN THE WAKE
OF THE
GREEN STORM

We shall not cease from exploration, and the end of all our exploring will be to arrive where we started and know the place for the first time.
—T.S. Eliot

THE SUN WAS A BURNING ORB in the blue heavens, and the temperature was 98 degrees.

Summer had at last returned. I was home in Shoreview. *Persistence* was on her trailer and safely perched on my driveway, drying out.[1]

Weather was never far from my mind. When I was not

working on my boat, I was in my air-conditioned office, rif-
fling through the media coverage of the spectacular storm I'd
been in.

Until now, I'd been hearing experiences from the boaters
themselves, but clearly I'd been out of touch. The Fourth of
July storm had been front-page news.

Studying newspaper photographs and articles, I was getting
a new perspective on what had come out to sea to hit me.

The storm had not begun somewhere up near the Canadian
border north of me, as I originally had thought, but along a sta-
tionary boundary on the western part of Minnesota. It then
moved eastward. Trees snapped, power lines went down in
winds clocked as high as 91 m.p.h.

Even in its earliest form, it was a nasty business. The storm
had torn roofs from buildings and flipped over airplanes and
even semi-trailer trucks. Torrential rains and flash flooding
forced some people from their homes. It closed roads, leaving
some cars underwater.

About 80 miles or so to the north and west of where I had
been, the Boundary Waters Canoe Area Wilderness (BWCAW)
had caught the worst of the storm's impact. Here the windstorm had devastated about a half a million acres, damaging 25
million trees.

Trees had been broken by straight-line winds like so many
matchsticks and were stacked as high as 10-feet deep.

It was "one of the largest North American forest distur-
bances in recorded history," a Minneapolis *Star-Tribune* article
reported.

"Wild downdrafts" resulted in "one of the biggest blow
downs ever recorded," wrote Paul Douglas,[2] weather forecast-
er for the *Star-Tribune.*

Like "Paul Bunyan went on a rampage with his ax,"
Minnesota Rep. Jim Oberstar[3] was quoted in the *St. Paul
Pioneer Press.* "You cannot imagine the destructive force until
you've seen it in person."

With wind gusts reported at "up to 100 miles per hour," the
newspapers called it the "the storm of the century."

I read with empathy as campers told that they felt as if they were in "a blender" as they hunkered under trees, listening to the sounds of tall pines snapping and falling

As search crews penetrated the wilderness area to look for survivors, they found several dozen people with injuries. In all, 19 people had to be evacuated from the BWCAW. It was only when the storm blew east across Lake Superior that an 11-year-old Wisconsin camper died from injuries

No doubt about it. The Independence Day windstorm had been severe before it moved out onto the lake.

* * *

I began checking the Internet. On the Web site of the Minnesota Department of Natural Resources (DNR), I saw a satellite map of the damage to the Boundary Waters Canoe Area wilderness. (www.ra.dnr.state.mn.us.bwca/sdav). The remarkable map showed a comparison of resource satellite images taken before and after the blowdown, which identified the extent of the damage. The heavy damage was shown in red in BWCAW, but the red spots continued to march to the east and to the lake where I was sailing.

In a related link from the Gunflint Ranger District, Grand Marais, Minnesota (http://snf.toofarnorth.org) explained that the storm was a "derecho."

"Every year we hear or read about hurricanes that march through the Gulf of Mexico or along the Atlantic Coast sweeping clear a large path. Mid-America, the area around and including Oklahoma, is known as 'tornado alley' and is a regular witness to the swift and deadly actions of tornadoes, developed from large thunderstorm cells, that wipe neighborhoods clean leaving only the foundations of homes and a little evidence of past occupation." These were derechos.

A derecho, I learned, is a convective windstorm consisting of not one but a complex of thunderstorms — a rare occurrence.

Toofarnorth said that "Northern Minnesota experienced a derecho on July 4, 1999 — a widespread convective windstorm consisting of a complex of thunderstorms."

The Fourth of July storm began with unstable air with high temperatures and dew points — warm and humid. The boundary stretched from north South Dakota northeasterly to International Falls, Minnesota, and east from there to near Thunder Bay, Canada. Out of this, a large complex of thunderstorms developed in South Dakota, accelerating and moving easterly and up into northern Minnesota. Record high winds were recorded at 91 m.p.h.

Rapidly, the storm system moved into north central Minnesota with winds speeds clocked as high as 90 m.p.h. per hour.

Trees bent over or napped off above the root systems; power lines went down. The web site reported, "In the Boundary Waters Canoe Area Wilderness, there is an area about 30 miles long and three to five miles wide of near complete downed, broken off and bent over trees — truly the worst of the storm's impact."

The straight-line winds had cut a swath through the Superior National Forest that caused a blowdown of about 477,000 acres of the National Forest.

It had taken only 30 minutes.

*   *   *

In the city of Thunder Bay, Ontario, residents were awed with the violent thunderstorm and the high winds — but especially the green sky.

Thunder Bay Meteorologist David Baggaley explained the phenomena. He pointed out that when that the sun shines on the top of the clouds it gets "refracted down — just like a prism," with the result being a green color comes through."

In Canada, the windstorm came to be called "The Green Storm.

*   *   *

The winds surged over the mountains, funneled by the Sleeping Giant mountain, and roared outward onto the bay and Superior's open waters — where they found me.

At Ontario Climate Center, Environment Canada, Bryan Smith confirmed that at the Trowbridge (Island) automatic weather station, "Peak wind from northwest gusting to 115 kph, i.e., hurricane force."Hurricane force! No wonder my little boat was blown around so much.

But no news reports told of what happened to boaters, those few who were out there, on the open waters of the lake, alone and exposed to the storm's fury.

I put down my papers.

I could tell them.

AUTHOR'S NOTES

Chapter 2

1/ I began building *Persistence* in 1978 beside my home in Shoreview, Minnesota., laying up her 20-foot hull in three layers of 1/8-inch thick veneers of western red cedar, in a triple diagonal pattern. Each veneer is held in place with a coating of boat-building epoxy glue. Her stringers are Sitka spruce (for lightness), fastened to composite mahogany ribs. When I had three veneer layers built up, I faired the hull, sanded it down, and wrapped it in fiberglass. Below the waterline, I added graphite powder to the epoxy and rolled on that mix to add additional toughness to the bottom. Above the waterline, the hull is bright finished with many coats of varnish over the transparent fiberglass and epoxy. The result is a deep piano-like varnish finish to an ultralightweight hull. The boat building took seven years.

2 / On one trip to Superior, I had broken an outboard at the start of a voyage. Backing down a primitive ramp, a trailer wheel sunk into a pothole, and the outboard motor jolted down. Its bottom had caught in the hole and the engine broke off and fell in the water. Loss of my engine nearly ruined my voyage. For more details, see *Call of the North Wind*.

3/ In *Persistence's* cabin, I have 46 inches of headroom. On either side of the 18-inch high open centerboard trunk, there are two aisles, each 71 inches long and 18 inches in width. To port, you have the navigation sta-tion; to starboard, you'll find the galley area. The way I get around below decks is either to sort of crawl or duckwaddle.

Chapter 3

1/ It was on a voyage in 1984 in *Persistence* that I was caught on this shore with a quick-rising storm with fierce winds and high seas — a dreaded northeaster. Without a nearby harbor of refuge or a marina to duck into, to get off the lake, I found that this was indeed a long stretch of bold and inhospitable shoreline.

Chapter 5

1/ Before he joined the National Park Service, Cooper was an underwater archeologist at the Underwater Archeology Program at the State Historical Society of Wisconsin, Madison, and well known for his studies of shipwrecks on Lake Superior. I consulted with him when I wrote about the wreck of the *Pretoria*, one of the most colossal wooden vessels in the world and maybe the biggest wooden ship ever built, in my book, *Call of the North Wind*. He'd dived many times on the bones of this 338-foot long goliath, wrecked in a storm and lying off Outer Island in the Apostle Islands.

2/ They traveled in brigades. After the voyageurs left New France (Montreal), their wilderness route led up the Ottawa, though Lake Nipissing, down the French River into Georgian Bay, across the top of

Lake Huron, around the falls at Sault Ste. Marie and into Lake Superior. Here they headed westward along the great northern arc of the lake to Grand Portage. Their arrival is described by John Macdonnell in 1793:

"Before arrival the voyageurs donned their finery and the brigades raced across Grand Portage Bay. Leaving point Au Pere we paddle two pipes (intervals between smoking breaks) and put to shore to give the men time to clean themselves, while we breakfasted — this done a short pipe brought us to Point au Chapeau (Hat Point) around which we got a sight of the long wished for Grand Portage. The beach was covered with spectators to see us arrive, our canoe went well and the crew sang paddling songs in a vociferous manner."

3/ Ten paddlers in a north canoe were able to ferry up to three tons of freight across Superior from the Sault to Grand Portage in less than 12 days, weather permitting. They got up before dawn and paddled until dusk and ate a ration of sagamite, which was bear grease and corn boiled in lye and described by an outsider as "tasting like wall paste." An easy day's journey was 30 miles, but if the weather and the wind were favorable, they could paddle up to 50 miles a day. If the storms came up, or the lake got rough, they also were prepared to sit out being "wind bound" for days.

4/ A voyageur's attitude was remarkable. Interviewed when he was an old man, a voyageur explained: "I could carry, paddle, walk, and sing with any man I ever saw. No water, no weather, ever stopped the paddle or the song. I had twelve wives in the country; and was once possessed of fifty horses, and six running dogs. I spent all my earnings in the enjoyment of pleasure. Five hundred pounds, twice told, have passed through my hands; although now I have not a spare shirt to my back, nor a penny to buy one. Yet were I young again, I should glory in commencing the same career again. There is no life so happy as a voyageur's life!"

Chapter 6

1/ Designed for offshore ocean use, the *Grampa Woo* was built in 1980 and hauled workers and equipment out on stormy waters to Gulf of Mexico oil rigs. Later, she made regular trips on the East Coast as a charter fishing boat and as a whale watcher. When Captain Dana located her, he converted her to take passengers out on cruises on the North Shore of Lake Superior. She was Kollar's million dollar retirement plan, and he and his wife, ChunAe, were so proud of her that they named her for ChunAe's much loved Korean father.

2/ The *Grampa Woo* had ended her first season on the North Shore and Dana was doing maintenance work, servicing her engines, and also outfitting her for her trip south. She was at Dana's mooring in Grand Portage Bay off Grand Portage Island, rather than at her regular dock at Beaver Bay about 150 miles to the south. Captain Dana had planned to go east toward Sault Ste. Marie, and then, exiting the Great Lakes, get on the rivers leading south to the Gulf of Mexico.

3/ Six months earlier, Dana had ordered a new set to replace the *Woo's* three mismatched propellers. On the port was a 30-inch diameter 32-pitch four-bladed propeller. Her center prop was 30-inch diameter, 31-pitch three-bladed. But the starboard was 32-inch diameter, 32-pitch four bladed. Because the wheels were mismatched, the port engine worked under a heavy load and ran at a higher temperature than the others. With a 2,400-mile trip to the Gulf, Dana wanted matched props that would let his engines pull an equal load, giving his beloved Woo better speed and economy with less vibration. The prop's expected delivery date had been September 1, but Dana said he got an explanation that the foundry in Mexico was just casting them. Weeks later, when he checked again, he was told the props had been held up in customs. Still later, he was told the props had been misplaced in shipment. After waiting nearly 60 days past the expected delivery date, the shipping company called to say the props were enroute, and, at his request, had faxed a notification of the delivery date. When he got written confirmation, Dana sent divers underwater in the chilly bay to take the propellers off the *Woo*. On October 30, the *Woo* was without propellers — her shiny shafts awaiting the new, matched props.

4/ The *Grampa Woo* was moored several hundred feet on the bay side of Grand Portage Island and tethered to the bottom by a hundred feet of heavy chain and 120 feet of one-and a half-inch thick line. Dana had put the mooring in: a massive 4,000 chunk of steel, on which re-rod spikes were welded. Some local sailors had jokingly told him his mooring was "over engineered."

5/ Inside the harbor and behind the island, the *Woo* would get protection from the northeast winds that can sweep the length of the lake and pile up huge waves. The mooring also was protected from northwest and southwest winds. But the wind this morning was blowing out of the west — howling along the rugged North Shore, across the spit of land guarding the harbor, and exiting the gap between Grand Portage Island and Hat Point. As Dana later recalled, if the wind had blown from nearly any other direction, the *Woo* would have gone into shallow water and survived, or, another way, ended up on a reef, but afloat. Only a 20 degree difference of direction would have saved her.

6/. In their haste to get to the *Woo*, they did not don special clothing or carry a radio to get help. They had jumped aboard the small inflatable in their shore-side clothing, protected only by light jackets, and were exposed to the heavy sweep of the wind and doused by waves in the bay. When the outboard engine began spluttering and nearly died, Dana realized that, given the direction the wind was blowing, they would have been swept out past Hat Point and into the stormy waters of Superior, and probably would have perished. He later told me the Zodiac ride was one of the two times during the ordeal that he was most frightened.

7/ Superior becomes deep quickly.

In a matter of minutes, the bottom under the *Woo* became 80, then 120 feet; finally, the depth sounder did not register the depth — it was too great.

8/ The captain of the *McCarthy* initially requested that Dana and Robin leave the *Grampa Woo* and board the ore boat. Dana recalled later, "In my heart I thought I owed my vessel the opportunity to get a tow." Both sailors elected to stay with their boat.

9/ If the *Woo* sank, Dana and Robin could take to a life raft. But this was a floatation tube with an open mesh bottom, more suited to summer cruises rather than autumn gales, so passengers sat in icy waters. There was no topside protection. Alerted to the danger, a U.S. Coast Guard rescue helicopter was standing by to be dispatched from Traverse City, Michigan — across the lake. But the flight over the stormy waters would take a couple of hours, and rescuers would have difficulty locating the downed sailors in the high seas and darkness.

10/ With the loss of the sea anchor, the *Grampa Woo* was no longer bow to the seas but cocking broadside to the waves, a dangerous position for any vessel. She was rolling in the troughs, presenting her vulnerable sides to the onrushing waves. Heavy weather storm tactics call for angling the bow or the stern to combat big waves.

11/The *Glenada* was skillfully maneuvered so that both she and the *Woo* were in the troughs of the waves, with both boats rising and falling at the same frequency. The captain gunned the engine to pinion her against the *Woo* so Dana and

Robin could jump to the *Glenada's* bow, about three or four feet higher than the *Woo's* railing. This was the second time, Captain Dana later told me, he experienced "real fear."

12/ After they had pulled into the safe harbor, Dana and Robin had to borrow dry clothes. As they stripped out of their wet suits, Dana saw Robin pull a damp, brown-colored object from the inside of his jacket. "What's that?" Dana had inquired. Robin grinned as he answered, "Oatmeal." When they abandoned ship, Robin had made a stop below to scoop up the teddy bear. Oatmeal, a special memento of a former girlfriend, thus became the third survivor of the *Woo*.

13/ The *Glenada's* crew was awarded the Governor General's Medal of Bravery, one of the highest accolades Canada can bestow. The Thunder Bay Coast Guard crew received commendations for seamanship and bravery in what was described as "one of the most harrowing at-sea rescues in recent Great Lakes History." The old *Wesfort* was replaced with a bigger, more powerful 47-foot Motor Lifeboat designed to perform as a heavy weather patrol and rescue craft.

14/ The route across the U.S. from Lake Superior to the Gulf of Mexico follows three Great Lakes, half a dozen states, and several rivers and waterways. Coming up from the Gulf of Mexico, *Grampa Woo II* entered the Tombigbee Waterway in Mobile, Alabama, went north on the Tennessee River to the Ohio River, in Kentucky, cruised southwestward a short distance on the Ohio River, entered the Mississippi River at

Cairo, Illinois, and cruised north-ward. Up from St. Louis, Missouri, she entered the Illinois River and sailed to Chicago. Here she entered Lake Michigan, cruised northward the length of the Great Lake, crossed over to Lake Huron, swung west-ward to the locks at Sault Ste. Marie, and then sailed westward on Lake Superior to the North Shore. On board, and in a special place of honor, was the ship's mascot, "Oatmeal."

Chapter 8

1/ The weather forecast originated from the upper peninsula of Michigan, on the other side of the lake. I tried to get the Canadian weather forecast out of Thunder Bay, but because of the hills and the weather, nothing was coming into my boat at Grand Portage but blurts of white noise.

2/ I wanted the boat's ends to be as buoyant as possible and any extra weight to be down low. Since I did not have a ballast keel below me, but merely a centerboard, I reasoned that any additional weight as low as I could get it would help. The stuff I took out of the forepeak and aft quar-ter berths included tools, supplies, canned food, water jugs, a clothing duffel bag, and books. I took out the floorboards, stacked everything as low as possible directly in the bilge, and piled it up both sides of the wooden centerboard trunk. Everything was strapped in place with bungee cords. The 3/8-inch steel centerboard was in full down position.

3/ Before I left Grand Portage, I

telephoned Jim Coslett, who I hoped to meet at Silver Islet. Now in his 80s, that grand old man of sailing had boated just about everywhere on the Canadian north shore. "You should visit Thompson Cove," he suggested.

4/ Later, I learned that Sue at Voyageur's Marina had been trying to warn me of a storm that had hit them with rain and high winds. I hadn't heard her radio call because of the onrushing storm's interfer-ence.

5/ I had put my fenders in the cock-pit because I was nearing Thompson Cove and I wanted them handy to drop alongside when I came into dock. They were heavy, six-inch diameter by 18-inch-long white rub-ber. I had placed them on my star-board cockpit seat, along with some line for tying up. The wind picked them up and whipped them away. I watched them fly out, one by one, and go skipping down the lake.

Chapter 9

1/ I later found that a stainless steel hook that held the shock chord secur-ing the mainsail had snapped off. The hook had been riveted to the boom.

Chapter 10

1/ This was only the second time water had come in through the open centerboard trunk. On August 17, 1998, I was tied up inside the Bayfield, Wisconsin, breakwall, near the entryway, when the wind began gusting to 35 knots down the west channel. I was making my usual morning latte when a heavy surge hit us, shoving us forward. I saw a big, green gulp of water fly upward from the centerboard trunk, climb halfway to the cabin top, and slop out. That day, in the surge, I broke two new three-eighths-inch diameter braided mooring lines.

Chapter 11

1/ The city of Thunder Bay, Ontario, lies about 18 miles north of Thompson Island and about 64 kilometers (40 miles) from the U.S. and Canada border and 175 miles north from Duluth, Minnesota. With a population of 113,662, Thunder Bay is the largest city on Lake Superior (Duluth, Minnesota, has a population of 85,493 and Superior, Wisconsin, 27,519). Thunder Bay has a beautiful setting opposite the Sleeping Giant Mountain and a huge, glistening waterfront and natural harbor. The largest freshwater port in the world, it is located at Mile Zero of the Saint Lawrence Seaway, about 2,235 miles by water from the Atlantic Ocean and 1,900 miles from the Pacific. I'd sailed into Thunder Bay in 1984 and spent several delightful weeks living aboard Persistence in Thunder Bay's Prince Arthur's Landing Marina. I wrote about this in my book, *In the Teeth of the Northeaster.*

2/ "Dense fog again," Gillian Rowe later described her return trip. "John had plotted the course into the southern break wall of the (Thunder Bay) harbor and entered waypoints into the GPS. The fog was dense (and) we did see the break wall as we passed, but were amazed we couldn't see the shore at all, even though it was so

close. The towering elevators that dominate the shoreline were completely blanketed."

3/ To make latte on my one-burner stove, I filled a cup-sized camping espresso maker full of water, filled the coffee container with espresso coffee (preground) and set it atop my stove. I use two metal cups, each with a big dollop of powdered skim milk, extra strong. These are filled about halfway with water. One is placed under the curved spigot of the espresso maker; soon the hot liquid comes bubbling up and into the cup. At about the halfway point for the espresso, I quickly switch cups and fill the second cup. The result? Two fine cups of espresso coffee with hot milk. To a purist, this isn't really a latte with hot, steamed milk, but on the other hand, it isn't bad. In its March 1997 issue, *Cruising World* published my article on making latte on a small sailboat. The article was entitled, *Little Things Mean A Latte.*

The author with espresso maker in *Persistence's* cabin

4/ Lynn later told me that at times they heeled 35 to 40 degrees as they got out of the lee of Pie Island and started the open crossing of the

Thunder Cape to Silver Islet. They recorded winds at a steady 24 to 27 miles per hour, but their heavy displacement cutter handled well. They dropped the main and sailed only under the jib to Silver Islet. "No matter how many times we venture by Pie and Sleeping Giant," he said, ominously, "we have always had a beast of a time with wind and wave."

Chapter 12

1/ Doug Irwin, captain of *Chris "N" Me*, is a Thunder Bay firefighter. Clive Dudley, captain of the *Lucky Lady*, is a self-employed Thunder Bay denturist. The rest of the group of six men from Thunder Bay in the two powerboats were all firefighters, with the exception of one man who is a service station owner. They are all old friends from Thunder Bay and meet during the winter in what they call their boat meetings, which Irwin says "involves a few jugs of draft." He explains: "We spend about five minutes planning and setting dates, then it's time to relax. Our wives realize that it takes a lot of meetings to get these trips organized."

2/ The hose tower is where the Thunder Bay firemen dry out their wet hoses.

3/ Clive approached the capsized boat on the leeward side, then came up so that the people in the water "blew into you." He explained the leeward (as opposed to the windward) is "the best way to do it. If you can do that, they'll come to you, rather than you crashing into them. Besides, their boat was over, and not knowing the rigging or what might be free on the windward side, it was safer to go up on the leeward side."

Chapter 13

1/ The Pukaskwa Pits have been regarded as one of Superior's archeological mysteries and have been the subject of controversy. About 250 of the mysterious depressions have been found along the water's side of Pukaskwa National Park, and archaeologists have dated some of these back as far as 1,000 B.C. Most are found on cobble beach, raised above the Big Lake's waterline, marking an earlier age when the water level was much higher. The original pits, brought to public attention in 1949, are named after the Pukaskwa River. In turn, the river is said to have been named after Joe Pukaskwa, who killed his wife, Sarah, and threw her burned ashes and bones into the river.

2/ Spirit quests, or vision quests, by Native Americans involve fasting for days until the seeker sees a vision that reveals secrets to him. On Superior, they are conducted in remote, lonely places in which nature seems overpowering.

3/ On Canada's eastern shore, early sailors to the New World placed their skin-clad boats atop stone foundations and lived under them. Canadian author Farley Mowat (*Cry, Wolf*, and *The Farfarers*) tells of staying ashore under an overturned canoe, with a tarpaulin pegged down on the high side to provide additional protection, in a fair degree of comfort and ease while wind-bound.

Chapter 14

1/ Tee Harbor, in the shadow of the Sleeping Giant, is where Capt. Dana and his rescuers spent the night after the loss of the *Grampa Woo*. The wide stretch of open water I just crossed between the island chain and the Sleeping Giant was where the last battle of the *Grampa Woo* had taken place. I wondered how this wild area — the high cliffs of the Sleeping Giant to the northeast and the vast openness of Superior to the south — must have appeared to the desperate sailors that nearly fatal night.

2/ Opposite Tee Harbor, to the south of the Giant, is the Trowbridge Island Light station. I could make out the high round structure and an adjacent building clearly atop the rocks as I made my turn to come to the aid of the sailboat on the reefs. It was here the steamer *Theano* met its end in a gale that suddenly blew up. In the November 1906 storm, snow was heavy and the waves huge, and the *Theano* crashed into the island's rocks and began filling with water. The crew went to its two lifeboats, and one sailor wrote: "The trip across Thunder Bay was the most terrible I have ever experienced. One minute it seemed that we were 20 feet above the surface and the next we would be on the crest of a gigantic wave with the bow of our boat pointing downward. Again and again waves would break over us drenching every man to the skin." The lifeboat crew finally returned to the city of Thunder Bay, "numbed, exhausted and almost overcome by exposure." They had been lucky. The next day, when a tug managed to get out to the rocks, the *Theano* was missing.

3/ They were not the only ones to go aground in this area. In the terrible storm of November 1905, the freighter *Monkshaven* had battled its way across Superior and was nearing the entryway to Thunder Bay. Wind-driven snow filled the air; the waves had grown deadly when Angus Island suddenly appeared. The vessel ran up on the craggy rock, ripping out its bottom. As the *Monkshaven* sank astern, its bow high on the island, crewmembers jumped ashore, only to realize that they were marooned on a wind-swept island in freezing cold and snow. They built a shelter on the island, and for three days, as the bow of the ship groaned above them, they huddled together in misery, convinced they were about to die. When the weather cleared a little on the fourth day, they clambered back aboard their ship for food and clothing. While some of the crew stayed on board, 13 boarded the ship's yawl and sailed toward Thunder Bay. Eventually a freighter picked them up. All were eventually rescued.

Not so lucky seven years later was the *Leafield*. In 60-m.p.h. winds and driving snow, the 250-foot, steel ocean-steamer fought her way toward Thunder Bay. Off Angus Island, she was seen to crest a giant wave — and then vanish. Her hull has never been found.

Chapter 15

1/ Silver Islet lies in the shadow of the Sleeping Giant. In Thunder Bay, you can easily make out the mountain's namesake, the giant's head, his Adam's apple, his chest, his knees, and the feet. Thunder Cape lies below the feet. The Sleeping Giant is so named, in Ojibwa legend, because after he gave away the secret of a vast silver horde to white men, the Great Spirit turned him into a mountain of stone.

2/ News of the rich find spread internationally. Europe was wild with stories of Superior's mineral riches, but few wanted to invest money in a rock in the middle of a lake — no matter how great its potential. Wrestling silver from under water seemed impossible.

3/ A coffer dam surrounded the shaft itself, but one miner during a storm saw "to our horror the waves rushing right through the middle of the island between the machinery house and shaft of the mine and boarding house. We saw two buildings go down before the waves...dense clouds of spray shot up against and over the houses, shops, and steam house, threatening to engulf them. The waves poured over the destroyed breakwater, carrying logs and stones upon their crests."

4/ Some enterprising miners tied choice chunks of silver ore onto pieces of wood, and when the wind was right, let them float across to Burnt Island where they hoped to recover them.

They didn't get all the silver; Ann Drynan spent many pleasant hours searching along the island's south shores. I acquired a lovely chunk of silver she had recovered. This was cut in half, and the flat side polished to show the silver ore.

5/ At the height of the silver boom, Silver Islet was one of the richest silver mines in the world, and speculation for Canadian silver was rampant. Speculators began sinking shafts in other islands, including Angus Island (opposite Pie Island); on Pie Island (so-named because it reminded French voyageurs of a French pastry), and on south McKellar Island.

Thompson Island's shaft was dug in speculation by the Montreal Mining Company in 1873, perhaps trying to reclaim some of the success it had before it prematurely sold Silver Islet — perhaps the worst financial judgment of the era.

6/ For a look at a model of Silver Islet, visit the Interpretive Center at the nearby Sleeping Giant Provincial Park. In this modernistic log and stone building is a six-foot-tall cutaway panorama of the mine at its peak operation. At eye level is the surface of Lake Superior where you can view the islet with boats docked on a pleasant day. You also can see the main operations of the mine, including the shaft house and pump house.

But cut your eyes downward to get a feel for the scope of what was once the world's richest silver mine. Here is the 1,200-foot-deep shaft with side tunnels running horizontally. In huge, underground caverns, miners balance themselves atop long ladders, picking away at the ore, their work illuminated by the flickering head candle lanterns.

"The mine is to scale," park superintendent Cam Sims told me. "And we got it right."

Chapter 16

1/ I set my depth sounder at 4 feet 6 inches, which is the depth of my boat with the centerboard fully down. If I retract the centerboard into its trunk, I have about 12 inches of depth before my keel bottoms out. However, my rudder extends below the water's surface about three feet.

2/ Later, I learned from the Bradfords aboard *Timothy Lee* that they had registered wind speeds of up to 45 m.p.h.

Chapter 17

1/ I may have been quite safe in my little cove, but just to the north of me lies the wreck of the steamship *Neebing*, known as "the coffin ship." Built in 1892, the 193-foot steel steamer was so rusted that sailors joked she was held together by layers of paint. When the heavy seas of a September 1937 storm hit her, she struggled toward the island, but burst her boiler and sank so quickly that four men and the captain went down with her, trapped below deck. One man was shot out of a galley skylight by compressed air as the ship sank; he survived. The "coffin ship" lies about a quarter mile off the tip of Moss Island, in Nipigon Straight, in about 60 feet of water.

Chapter 18

1/ Lake Superior was down quite a bit this summer from its maximum level, set in 1984, of 603.1 feet. On my voyage, the lake level averaged 601.0 feet. That meant a lot of rocks would be bothering boaters.

2/ The centerboard was mild steel and held in the hull by a single three-quarters-inch diameter silicone bronze bolt pinioned through wood. In practice, the centerboard was a long-arm lever, exerting tremendous force on the wood. Something could crack, break, or come loose down there, and the thought of sleeping in, and sailing, a slowly sinking ship bothered me a lot.

3/ CPR Slip, also known as Squaw Harbour, was named after the Canadian Pacific Railway. In the early 1900s, the railroad had a lodge in Nipigon, Ontario, and brought wealthy guests out to cabins for fishing expeditions and a wilderness getaway. The camp was abandoned until volunteer boaters along the North Shore came out to put in wooden docks, walks, outdoor pit toilets, and several buildings.

4/ Lake Nipigon is a 20-mile long expanse of water that connects with Lake Superior and is to the north of St. Ignance and Simpson islands.

5/ Rossport, one of the most beautiful harbors on the Canadian North Shore, is located 108 miles east of Thunder Bay and 288 miles from Duluth. This friendly, but tiny town, was once a fishing village.

Chapter 19

1/ *Orenda's* hull is one-inch thick layers of Western Red Cedar (old growth), and from the waterline up is capped with three-eighths-inch thick hand-matched Honduras mahogany. The mahogany is only on the topsides and set at a 45-degree angle to the keel. Below the waterline, *Orenda's* massive keel is stainless steel filled with lead.

2/ Copyright 1976 by Moose Music, Inc. I had obtained permission to quote a few lines when I did my analysis of the last hours of the *Edmund Fitzgerald* and why she sank, in my book *In the Teeth of the Northeaster: A solo voyage on Lake Superior.*

3/ *WoodenBoat* is a national magazine for wooden boat builders and sailors. From time to time, some of my own writings have appeared in Peter Spectre's *On the Waterfront* section.

4/ Mike told me later that *Orenda* has a stainless steel stern ladder. However, they keep it below, out of sight, when they leave their boat at anchor. He joked to me that they use it "for swimmers, an unknown species in Lake Superior."

5/ I also had failed to see the natural harbor entryway from the seaward side of Thompson during the 4th of July Green Storm and had continued on to the eastern tip of the island, where I also encountered "the pass" and the wave-scoured string of smaller islands. Unlike Ed, I had plunged right on through — to my regret. See Chapter 9: *Fight to the Island.*

Chapter 20

1/ Built in 1906 and rated at 7,763 gross tons, the *Morrell* was 600 feet long, nearly 60 feet wide and drew 27 feet. She'd been outfitted with a new 3,200 horsepower steam engine in 1956 and had passed all the routine Coast Guard inspections. Her crew had confidence in her and thought she was a tough ship. She had been caught out in the 1958 Superior storm that had sunk the *Bradley*, another ore vessel, and had come through unscathed in 100-m.p.h. winds and high seas.

2/ A fall blizzard had descended, with high winds and stormy seas. The seas were confused, running both from the north-northeast and the north-northwest.

The captain aboard a following vessel, *the Edward Y. Townsend*, said the storm was the worst he had ever encountered on the Great Lakes.

3/ The raft was a wide-open floatation unit built of two eight-foot-long steel pontoons, topped with a flat decking of wooden planks. In the center of the raft was a compartment with emergency signaling gear. Since the raft was too heavy to pick up and throw overboard, it could only be launched if the bow section sank and the raft floated off. The ship did have lifeboats, but these were located in the aft section — unreachable to Dennis and his crewmates over the cracking hull.

4/ When he was under water, Dennis used an old scuba diver's trick to determine which way he had to go. He exhaled and followed the bubbles as they rose to the surface.

5/ According to the Marine Board of Investigation Report, Cleary and Stojek died around 0600 hours and Fossbender died at about 1600 hours. The first two men had endured about six hours of exposure, the third man, about 16 hours.

The cause of death was listed on their death certificates as drowning and that "exposure was an antecedent cause." Fossbinder had complained that his lungs were filling up from the foam and the spray. The report said that the men were all believed to be conscious until shortly before death. Hale later found out that although Fossbender never complained, his chest had been crushed and both shoulders were broken.

6/ By his own estimate, Dennis did not urinate for more than 24 hours.

7/ Dennis did not come through the ordeal unscathed. He lost 50 pounds and suffered damage to his left arm. His frostbitten feet were his biggest problem, and over a period of years, he had one operation on the right foot and ten on the left.

8/ The stern section of the *Morrell* lies at rest on the bottom of Lake Huron in about 200 feet of water. She had traveled about five miles under her own power before sinking. The bow section rests about 19 miles north of the tip of Michigan's "thumb."

9/ In their report, the Marine Board of Investigations pointed out that the steel used in the *Morrell* was "notch sensitive," meaning the old-style steel got brittle as it got colder and lost much of its strength. The board also pointed out that the vessel might have broached and sustained a hull fracture while attempting to hold into the seas or to regain her heading. The board ominously concluded that any ballasted vessel of a design similar to the *Morrell*

would suffer "severe stresses and strains in sea and wind conditions such as those present on 29 November should it remain in or at angles to the trough for any length of time." This conclusion was predicated upon the fact that a 600-foot vessel at an angle of approximately 30 degrees to seas having crests of 250 to 300 feet apart "will suffer severe hogging, sagging and twisting stresses."

Chapter 21

1/ Bowman Island, just north of Paradise Island, is about a mile and a half north of Talbot Island and northeast about two and a quarter miles from CPR Slip. Several boaters from CPR had visited the island and paid their respects at the white-painted wooden cross that marks the lighthouse keeper's grave.

2/ Years later, Canadian historians have gone over the island and found the foundations and, possibly, the rock cairn where Mrs. Lamphier stored her husband's body that one terrible winter.

3/ In 1823, Dr. John J. Bigsby was paddling through this area in a canoe. In his book, *Shoe and Canoe*, the good doctor wrote that Nipigon Bay is "full of enchanting scenery. As we journey up this great water we have the ever changing pictures presented by the belt of islands on our left; while on our right we have the Nipigon mainland, an assemblage of bold mounts from 900 to 1200 feet high, tabular, rounded, or in hummocks, or sugar loaf, and only separated by very narrow clefts or gorges. The bay is a beautiful lake of itself, so transparent that we can, for miles together, see its red pavement and living and dead things there inhabiting." The islands, he wrote: "are numerous ... and often very high ... worn by watercourses into singular shapes, such as pillars, arches, recesses ... and window-like apertures, which not a little resemble a street of ruined chapels and chantries shrouded by mosses, vines and forest trees."

Chapter 22

1/ The Apostles Islands National Lakeshore, a forested archipelago of 21 islands located on the south shore of Lake Superior, encompasses a 720-square-mile area off the Bayfield Peninsula. The Canadian archipelago of islands in which I was sailing — proposed for the world's largest freshwater conservation area — has an area of more than 10,700 square kilometers. "When you're on the lake around here and stop on one of the islands," Basher says, "you feel like you're Robinson Crusoe. If you find another footprint, you'd be surprised."

2/ Piver was an early designer of trimarans that had an early reputation for flimsiness and poor home-built construction. One Thunder Bay couple I had talked to were out on the bay one day in their tri when a storm arose out of the northeast. They turned their Piver around and began surfing downwind in the growing swells. One arma dug in and it pitch poled, end over end. In the near-freezing water, they pulled

themselves aboard the overturned hull, hastily wrapped themselves in a sail, and rode the boat to shore. There, they stepped off, chilled but unhurt.

Chapter 23

1/ When I checked my edition of *The Coast Pilot*, it warned "The channel should not be used at night or in low visibility ...."

2/ It was well-known to local fishermen and pilots, especially after a Rossport fisherman named Mc-Garvey had run his boat atop it. However, the reef was not shown on U.S. nautical charts.

3/ Grappling hooks are large, metal hooks meant to catch and hold onto anything below. They are employed from a surface ship and are used blindly. The grappling attempt on the *Gunilda* smashed the smokestack, pulled off some parts of the masts and rigging and clawed up parts of her superstructure. It also broke part of her long bowsprit.

4/ The story of the *Gunilda* and Fred Broennle, the original expedition organizer with Charles King Hague, is told in a 72-minute feature film, *Drowning in Dreams*, released by the National Film Board of Canada. The film shows some of the underwater camera work done by Broennle, including photography of the yacht's gold-gilded transom, a crystal chandelier, a grand piano, the beautiful mahogany paneling and fireplaces, and even a brass clock. More information and recent underwater photographs can be found at *www.gunilda.com*.

5/ "Actually, it's the topmast from

the *Gunilda*," Ned told me. "It had floated ashore some years ago, and somebody had stuck it under a garage. I bought it and thought it'd be better here."

6/ I had met Jean Pierre Cousteau when he had come up the Mississippi River to Saint Paul on board his wooden ship, the *Calypso*. The underwater explorers had spent some time on Superior, and I asked him about the *Gunilda*. They had sent their submersible down to see what she was like and he told me, with awe in his voice: "She's the most magnificently preserved wreck I've ever seen."

7/ Today's sport SCUBA divers make the dive breathing mixed gases (oxygen, helium and argon), which prevent nitrogen narcosis. They descend with the aid of a downline attached to the *Gunilda's* aft mast to the deck of the sunken ship. The water at those depths is only a few degrees above freezing, but it is clear with about 20 feet of visibility. Diving experts say ambient light is low, so some kind of battery-powered light is necessary.

8/ He said that only two to three groups of divers came up the previous year to go down on the *Gunilda*. It's a difficult, dark dive. "What spooks most divers," Basher said, "is that you don't see anything until 275 feet. Many wrecks have their bow in about 85 feet, but on the *Gunilda*, you don't see anything until nearly 275 feet."

Chapter 24

1/ The name Les Petits Ecrits means "the small writings," but none have been found here. On the steep cliffs, wrote Major Joseph Delafield, in a canoe trip with six voyageurs in 1823, are "... figured images of deer, moose, canoes, Indians with bows ... all pretty well delineated, some by Indians and some by voyageurs. The base of the rock is a red feldspar, so that when the rust and lichens which now cover them are rubbed off by a stone or iron, a bright red surface is produced which forms the images. (It is) the picture gallery of Lake Superior."

2/ Dr. John Bigsby, in an 1823 canoe voyage, wrote: "No one has spoiled the crystal purity of Lake Superior's waters, so transparent that small objects may be seen scores of feet below the surface, nor made them any warmer."

3/ I was at the end of the Slates' main island chain, between Mortimore and Paterson Island. Directly ahead, near the mouth of the channel, were several tiny islands; beyond, to the east lay the boundary line of the Canada's proposed National Maritime Conservation Area. I had completed my voyage, sailing pretty much all the way through this area, west to east.

4/ In my 1984 voyage into Thunder Bay, I had carried a clipping from the *Minneapolis Star Tribune* aboard *Persistence* which had the headline, "Gold! Cry Arises from Superior's North Shore." In Hemlo, I had visited the moose pasture that had become a gold field, complete with brightly colored, tall structures that looked like a transplanted part of a North Sea oil rig. There were no big lumps of precious metal to be found — the stuff the early miners looked for, but found only on Silver Islet — but only minute traces. The gold ore they mined along the North Shore was seventeen one hundreths of an ounce up to thirty-two hundreths of an ounce per ton — a fraction of an ounce per ton, a microscopic quantity. Yet the Canadians did it with computers and high tech gear, producing an awesome amount of gold. "Where can I find some?" I inquired. The miner smiled patiently and told me I had passed right by a large outcropping of gold bearing rock — and had not recognized it.

5/ I felt especially privileged to see one of these majestic creatures. I had been told there was a goodly population here in the Slates, and that I might see one if I were lucky. The Slates are the haunts farthest south of these great beasts of the Arctic Circle.

6/ Albert Leon built his masterpiece, a 60-foot schooner by the name of *Perseverance*, at Old Fort William, where he was the shipwright. It was a replica of a Superior boat that had been used in the fur-trading days, and he had personally researched the plans and the building techniques. Working only with old-fashioned tools and dressed in traditional shipwright's gear, he shaped native woods, plank by plank. I had been on the *Perseverance* several times and was amazed he could build so large a craft with only hand tools. When it was finished, its tall masts raked the sky as it floated on the Kaministikwia River, flowing in front of the old fur fort along the

voyageurs' "fur highway." Albert had plans to sail it in a historic voyage around the Great Lakes, but after several years, the ship was sold to another museum. Albert retired.

Chapter 25

1/ The Three Sisters had also visited me. I was sailing on Minnesota's North Shore in my twenty-foot centerboard sloop, *Persistence*. For my account of meeting the Three Sisters off Castle Danger, see the chapter, *Storm over Superior*, in my book *In the Teeth of the Northeaster*.

2/ In a storm with 30-foot waves and 80-m.p.h. winds, the 739-foot *Edmund Fitzgerald* sank on November 10, 1975, in 539 feet of water off Michigan's Shipwreck Coast, with a loss of all hands. I reconstructed her last hours in the chapter *The Mystery of the Edmund Fitzgerald* in *In the Teeth of the Northeaster*. After I sailed the Shipwreck Coast, and close by her final resting place, I did a follow-up chapter on the *Fitzgerald* in my book *Call of the North Wind*.

Chapter 26

1/ These days, a new *Beef* is jauntily tied alongside Superior Charters. At first glance it looks exactly like the old *Beef*, but the new boat has a white hull with red trim. The engines are different, also, with two new and more powerful 150-h.p. Johnson outboards.

Dave had found exactly the boat he wanted.

The new *Beef* is a 23-foot Seacraft hull — identical to the old one.

"Best heavy weather vessel in that size range ever made," Dave emphasized.

Chapter 27

1/ It's called Whiskey Island because it was used during the days of the CPR railroad construction as a place to store bootleg whiskey for a thriving, but illegal whiskey trade for workmen. The CPR line around Superior, part of a coast-to-coast railroad line, was completed in 1885. In contrast, the Trans-Canada Highway around Superior's Canadian north shore was only completed in 1960.

2/ Rumors were flying that actor Mel Gibson had purchased a large, spectacular house along Minnesota's North Shore. Like the other Mel rumors, including the star's yacht on Superior, it proved to be untrue.

3/ The Hollywood actor-director and his wife have seven children, the latest delivered early in 1999. Gibson won an Oscar in 1996 for directing "Braveheart."

4/ GPS stands for Global Positioning System. It's a hand-held unit that contains an antenna, receiver, and processor, which reads signals from satellites orbiting the Earth about 10,900 nautical miles high. Onboard *Persistence*, I carried a Magellan GPS 2000 XL, which I bought for less than $150 at a discount marine supply store.

5/ The *Duluth News-Tribune* carried a story about the baggy encounter. The columnist for "Eh" had called Ned Basher, who apparently was enjoying a bit of northwoods humor when he said that Halcyon Harbor's Rose Renaud had actually sorted through the baggies and had found something that identified the catamaran as belonging to Gibson. But following up on the scoop, the Duluth news writer got in touch with Rose, who vehemently denied picking through the bags — but complained that they had to pay for the boat's trash. "They dumped 20 bags on us," she was quoted as saying, "and didn't drop any money to go with it, eh."

Chapter 28

1/ Both Joe and Rick were veteran Superior boaters, who, on the way to Loon Harbor, had gone aground on a reef. They told me their story: Aboard their 32-foot Island Packet, *Manitou*, Rick and Carol Munsinger of Omaha were startled when they heard, "thump, thump" — and their boat stopped, dead in the water. The *Manitou* had gone up on the rocks near Dreadnought Island, about three-quarters of a mile off Porphyry Island.

"Small island, big reef," Rick said. "I thought I was hard aground." He dropped his sails — they were pushing his boat further onto the reef — and got on the radio to his friends.

Joe and Elaine Floyd, of Eden Prairie, Minnesota, were following in their 40-foot Pacific Seacraft about three-fourths of a mile behind the *Manitou*.

The Floyds had seen their friends to port heading for green water.

They saw *Manitou's* mast roll forward and the boat come to a stop. In three-foot seas with water splashing aboard, Rick motored over in a dinghy to the *Hennessy*, got a 400-foot-long, three-fourths-inch diameter line, and hurried back to the aground *Manitou* to tie the boats together.

Hennessy's engine roared full forward and the 65-h.p. Yanmar dug in. Onboard the *Manitou*, Rick had his engine in full reverse.

"We just backed right off into deep water," Rick said. "Everyone on both boats just sat in silence," Joe told me, "as we pondered how bad the situation could have been."

"I came by a few days earlier," I said. "Navigating on GPS. I got around the reef OK."

Rick explained that he was navigating by Loran, "using the same waypoint I used last year. But we were getting weak signals. The Loran position was off and put me on the rocks. Now I have the Loran down — and the GPS up."

Rick added, "After my grounding, I compared my Loran to my GPS. The Loran was two and a half miles off course, and, it would have put me right through the center of the island."

He concluded: "I would have been in a world of hurt if nobody had been around."

2 / Despite the storm, Captain Kenney and his Iowa friends had had a wonderful time boating.

Later, I checked with the two sailboat captains, Rick and Joe, who reported they had reached the protection of the Slate Islands when the storm hit and hardly noticed it.

Chapter 30

1/ One of the first things I did was to crawl underneath the boat to look for damages and what might be causing my boat's persistent leak. I saw the hull's bottom had taken quite a beating.

Aside from various dings and scratches, hull material had been dug out where a big gouge traced itself across the portside bottom, from several feet back from the bow to the stub keel area.

Additionally, a big chunk of white oak keelson was missing, about six inches in length by about an inch thick.

The damage continued aft to the stub keel, where there was a deep gouge and oak splinters. The bottom forward tip was smashed. To one side of the stub keel was another deep gash.

Crawling directly underneath the centerboard trunk area, I peered upward, using the light of a flashlight. Here I saw epoxy-carbon flaking and chipping.

This was the source of the leak. I hadn't broken anything off, but apparently I had cracked the wooden case holding the centerboard bolt.

Fixing the boat would take time and effort. But I reminded myself that I had built the boat and that, after all, it was wood, wasn't it?

2/ I later asked Paul Douglas why Lake Superior brews up such wild storms.

He answered, "Because Lake Superior is so deep, it stays cold (as you know) well into the summer. This can create a huge differential in air temperature between the chilly waters and the relatively warm air passing overhead, increasing the odds of wild thunderstorms and high winds."

He added, "Of all the Great Lakes, I would LEAST want to be caught on Superior."

3/ When Rep. Obserstar visited the BWCAW following the storm, he likened the disaster to Washington's Mount St. Helen's eruptions. The Minnesota storm, he said, destroyed four times the number of trees downed by the volcano.

ACKNOWLEDGEMENTS

M Y SPECIAL THANKS to the Thunder Bay Coast Guard. I felt that as I cruised along the northernmost arc of the lake among the wilderness islands, that I always had a friend within radio call. I especially want to thank Brian Lane, Officer in Charge, for his many courtesies, particularly as I began planning my sail into Canadian Waters.

Special thanks to Clive Dudley, of Thunder Bay, for his contributions to this book and his knowledge of the lake, which he was kind enough to share. I wish him well in his work to restore the historic tugboat, *James Whalen*, in Thunder Bay. It was the *Whalen* that pulled the *Gunilda* off the reef near Rossport.

Doug Irwin, Thunder Bay, is another dedicated enthusiast of the Big Lake. His contributions to my understanding as a mariner are much appreciated.

Special thanks to Jim Coslett, Silver Islet, the grand old man of the lake, whose helpfulness and generosity are acknowledged.

For the many Thunder Bay, Ontario, and other Canadian boaters I met during my trip, I want to say that I appreciated the unusual courtesy and friendliness of sharing a harbor or an anchorage in their side of Superior — and their hospitality and their warmth. Not to mention a beer or two.

I can still recall arriving in Thompson Cove, thoroughly chilled to the point of near hypothermia and somewhat shaken that awesome July Fourth, and being helped by the Thunder Bay boaters. You were wonderful — and I won't forget it.

Let the name of Thunder Bay go down in the mariner roll calls of being among the boldest of boaters on the often rough waters they call their home — as well as being so wonderfully courteous and helpful.

If Superior is at times wild, cold and hard, her northern waterfront people are civilized, warm, and hospitable. I never felt that in any Canadian harbor, cove, or inlet that I poked my bow into that I lacked for help and support if I needed it.

I only hope this book has done justice to their wonderful spirit of Superior.

I especially want to thank Gail Jackson, whom I met on the docks at Silver Islet. As the program director, she provided me with information about the proposal new National Marine Conservation Area on Superior that I sailed through. With luck and commitment, this Lake Superior marine conservation area could be a reality in the next couple of years. I'd like that.

My special thanks to those boaters I met at various boat shows and at the various wooden boat festivals I attended for their collective information about voyaging along the Canadian North Shore. I enjoyed meeting them. They also filled in a lot of gaps in my knowledge on the Independence Day Green Storm.

Thanks to David Cooper, of the National Park Service, at Grand Portage, for his help both in person and later in helping me understand and appreciate the history of Grand Portage.

I would also like to thank my wife, Loris, and son, Will. I know that my absence during my voyage caused them pain and loneliness. I am most appreciative of their brave, loving support before, during, and after my voyage. Both Loris and Will read and contributed suggestions to this manuscript, though, as author, I alone bear the responsibility for its final outcome and accuracy.

I also want to thank the people whom I met and interviewed at length who took the time to review my material for accuracy and content. The book benefits from their insights and their inputs.

I am especially thankful for whatever powers that be that let me enter into this special world that is Superior and, equally important, to be able to bring back the material for this book.

— Marlin Bree

GETTING IN TOUCH WITH THE AUTHOR

I am happy to hear from readers and especially from people I met during my voyages.

The best way to reach me is e-mail. This address is:

marlin.marlor@minn.net

If you do not have e-mail, you can also the postal service and send your comments or information to:

Marlin Bree
Marlor Press
4304 Brigadoon Dr.
St. Paul, MN., 55126.

In general, I find it's a lot easier to read and tap out a reply (usually brief) on e-mail. It's a great way to stay in touch and to share thoughts and expereinces.

Comments on sailing, personal observations on the Big Lake, or thoughts on the author's books are welcomed, particularly, if you are a fellow boater who has sailed the same watery trail that I have.

But don't let that hold you back.

— Marlin Bree

SELECTED BIBLIOGRAPHY

Newspapers

Boxmeyer, Don. *No Port in a Storm. Saint Paul Pioneer Press,* November, 1996.

Boxmeyer, Don . *Home Port: A seafaring sequel: the voyage of the Grampa Woo III. Saint Paul Pioneer Press,* June 13, 1997.

Franklin, Robert. *Wind-swept BWCA facing new threats.* Minneapolis *Star Tribune,* July 8, 1999

Welsch, Chris, *After storm, wilderness transformed, and transforming.* Minneapolis *Star Tribune,* October 10, 1999

Books

Barr, Elinor, Silver Islet: *Striking it rich in Lake Superior,* Natural Heritage Books, 1988.

Bogue, Margaret Beattie, and Virgina A Palmer, *Around the Shores of Lake Superior: A Guide to Historic Sites.* Madison: University of Wisconsin Sea Grand College Program, 1979.

Bowen, Dana Thomas. *Memories of the Lakes.* Freshwater Press, Cleveland, Ohio, 1984

Boyer, Dwight, *Ghost Ships of the Great Lakes,* New York, Dodd, Mead, 1984.

Breining, Greg. *Wild Shore.* University of Minnesota Press, Minneapolis, 2000

Chishom, Barbara, and Gutsche, Andrea, *Superior: Under the Shadow of the Gods; A Guide to the History of the Canadian Shore of Lake Superior.* Lynx Images, Toronto, 1998.

Dahl, Bonnie. *The Superior Way: A Cruising Guide to Lake Superior.* Lake Superior Port Cities, Inc., Duluth, 1992

Department of Transportation Marine Board of Investigation. *SS Daniel J. Morrell, sinking with loss of life Lake Huron, 29 Nov 1966.* U.S. Coast Guard Marine Board of Investigation Report and Commandant's Action. Action by National Transportation Safety Board. March 4, 1968.

Dwyer, Jim. *Lake Superior Gold: An Amateur's Guide to Prospecting in the Lake Superior Region.* North Star Press of St. Cloud, Inc.,1953.

Folwell, William Watts. A History of Minnesota. Minnesota Historical Society, 1956

Hale, Dennis, as told to Jim Juhl, Pat & Jim Stayer. *Sole Survivor: Dennis Hale's Own Story.* Lakeshore Charters & Marine Explorations, Inc., Lexington, MI., 1996

Littlejohn, Bruce, and Wayland, Drew. *Superior: The Haunted Shore.*

Macmillan of Canada, Toronto,1983.

Marshall, Jim. *Shipwrecks of Lake Superior.* Lake Superior Port Cities, Inc., Duluth. 1987

National Oceanic and Atmospheric Administration, National Ocean Service, U.S. Dept. of Commerce. *United States Coast Pilot:* Great Lakes. Washington, D. C.,1984

Nute, Grace Lee. *Lake Superior.* Bobbs-Merrill Co., Indianapolis - New York, 1944. *This book has been with me aboard my boat on every voyage and is my favorite history book about Lake Superior.* The University of Minnesota Press had the uncommon good sense to reprint this book as a trade paperback in 2000.

Ratigan, William. *Great Lakes Shipwrecks & Survivals.* Galahad Books, New York. 1960

Ross, Alexander. *The Fur Hunters of the Far West.* London, 1855.

Scott, McWilliam. *Gunilda Shipwreck Survey & Assessment.* Brantford, Ontario. 1995.

Skelton, Joan. *Rescue from Grampa Woo.* Natural Heritage / Natural History. Toronto, 1998.

Stonehouse, Frederick, *Haunted Lakes: Great Lakes Ghost Stories, Superstitions and Sea Serpents.* Lake Superior Port Cities, Duluth, 1997.

Strathbogey, James. *Confessions of a Cornish Miner: Silver Islet: 1870 - 1884.* Porphry Press, Thunder Bay, 1987

Waters, Thomas F. *The Superior North Shore.* University of Minnesota Press, 1987

Woff Jr., Julius F. *Lake Superior Shipwrecks.* Lake Superior Port Cities, Inc., Duluth, 1990.

INDEX

J
Johnson, Sue, 41

K
Kenney, Ray, *Yennek*, 169 – 172, 187 - 188
Keyser, Mike, *Orenda*, 122 - 126
Kollars, Captain Dana, *Grampa Woo*, 27 - 38

L
Lake Superior National Marine Conservation Area Proposal
  General description, 6
  Persistence enters, 96
  Persistence exits, 166
  Map, 97
Leon, Albert, 165 - 166
Loon Harbor, 101 - 102

M
McCarthy, Walter J., 29 - 31
Melby, Kek, 18, 28 - 29
Moss Island, 107, 109
Munsinger, Rick, *Manitou*, 186

P
Persistence
  Boat repairs, 7 - 9
  Inside steering, 10
  Gear, 11
  In Green Storm, 43 - 56
  Aground, 112 - 114
  In fog, 142 - 145
Pukaskwa Pits, Thompson Island, 79 - 80

R
Reid, Cam, *Orenda*, 122 - 126
Rossport, 146, 147 – 148, 185
Rossport Inn, 149 - 151
Rowe, Gillian, *Capricorn II*, 65

S
Silver Islet, 82 – 84, 87 - 93

Simpson Strait, 143
Sivill, Robin, 28 - 37
Slate Islands, 159, 161 - 165
Sleeping Giant, 82
Spar Island, 46, 51
Superior, Lake, 14, 47
Swede Harbor, 99 - 100

T
Tee Harbor, 82
Thompson Cove, 45, 52, 56, 59
Thompson Island, 45, 52
Thunder Bay, 45, 66, 188
Thunder Bay Coast Guard, 31, 45, 58, 62, 110, 144
Titanic, 138

V
Voyageurs, 19 - 24
Voyageur's Marina, 15, 27, 40
Voyageur II, 40

W
Wesfort, 32
Whalen, James, 155
Woo, Grampa, 26 - 38
Wray, Al, 78 - 79

WIND SPEED
DESIGNATIONS

M.P.H.	DESIGNATION
13 – 18	Moderate winds
19 – 24	Fresh winds
25 – 31	Strong winds
32 – 38	Near gale
39 – 46	Gale
47 – 54	Strong gale
55 – 63	Storm
64 – 73	Violent storm
74 – 82	Hurricane

The above scale in miles per hour
is from the *Boat Log & Record*
and abbreviated from the
Beaufort Scale for Wind Force.

Photo / Will Bree

Marlin Bree, the author of *Wake of the Green Storm*, stands in the hatchway of his beloved wooden boat, *Persistence,* which he built himself. If someone asks how long it took to build his cedar-veneer hulled sailboat, he answers "seven years, and it's not done yet." He once lived along Lake Superior's shores and is an inveterate boater.

He is also the author of *Call of the North Wind*, and, *In the Teeth of the Northeaster: A Solo Voyage on Lake Superior.* He co-authored the national best-seller, *Alone Against the Atlantic*, with sailor Gerry Spiess. He developed the *Boat Log & Record.*

Bree is profiled in *Who's Who in America* and *The International Authors and Writer's Who's Who.* He is a former magazine editor for the Minneapolis *Star Tribune* and is a past president of the Minnesota Press Club.

When he is not sailing on Lake Superior, he boats in White Bear Lake, Minnesota. The author lives with his wife, Loris, son, Will, and ocicat, Tico, in Shoreview, Minnesota.